HISTORY OF THE RASHTRAKUTAS

HISTORY OF THE RASHTRAKUTAS

PANDIT BISHESHWAR NATH REU

Published by

Isha Books
B-63, Ist Floor
New Gupta Colony
Near DDA Market
Delhi - 110009

Distribution Network
gyanbooks.com
India, USA, Canada, UK, Australia

ISBN: 978-93-3285-217-4 (HB)

First Published, 1933

2nd Impression 2025

Printed at: Gyan Press, Delhi.

HISTORY OF THE RASHTRAKUTAS

Author: PANDIT BISHESHWAR NATH REU

Major His Highness Raj Rajeshwar Sramad Rajai Hind Maharajadhiraj Sri Sir Umaid Singhji Sahib Bahadur, G.C.I.E., K.C.S.I., K.C.V.O., Maharaja of Jodhpur.

HISTORY OF THE RĀSHTRAKŪTAS

(RĀṬHŌḌAS)

(From the beginning to the migration of Rao Sīha towards Marwar.)

HISTORY OF
THE RASHTRAKUTAS.

(RĀTHŌḌAS)

[From the beginning to the migration of Rao Siha towards Marwar.]

BY

PANDIT BISHESHWAR NATH REU,

Superintendent,

ARCHÆOLOGICAL DEPARTMENT & SUMER PUBLIC LIBRARY,

JODHPUR.

JODHPUR:

E ARCHAEOLOGICAL DEPARTMENT.

1933.

PREFACE.

This volume contains the history of the early Rāshṭrakūṭas (Rāṭhōḍas) and their well-known branch, the Gāhaḍavālas of Kanauj up to the third-quarter of the 13th century of Vikrama era, that is, up to the migration of Rāo Sīhā towards Marwar.

In the absence of any written account of the rulers of this dynasty, the history is based on its copper plates, inscriptions and coins hitherto discovered. Sanskrit, Arabic and English[1] works, which throw some light on the history of this dynasty, however meagre, have also been referred to. Though the material thus gathered is not much, yet what is known is sufficient to prove that some of the kings of this dynasty were most powerful rulers of their time. Further, some of them, besides being the patrons of art and literature, were themselves good scholars. The artistic and literary works of their time are held in high esteem even to this day.

The extent of their power is sufficiently vouchsafed by the writings of the early Arab travellers and the levying of "Turushkaḍaṇḍa" a tax like "Jaziā" on the Mohammedans, by Gōvindachandra.

Nor was their generosity less defined. Out of numerous copper grants recovered, no less than 42

1 Specially Sir R. G. Bhandarkar's article in the Bombay Gazetteer.

trace their source of munificence to a single donor, Gōvindachandra. Another magnificent example of their generosity is brought to light by a couplet from the copper grant[1] of Dantivarman (Dantidurga) II, dated Shaka Samvat 675 (V.S. 810=A.D. 753). The couplet runs as follows:—

मातृभक्तिः प्रतिग्रामं, ग्रामलक्षचतुष्टयम् ।
ददत्या भूप्रदानानि, यस्यमात्रा प्रकाशिता ॥ १६ ॥

i.e., His (Dantivarman's) mother by granting lands in charity in almost all the 400,000 villages of his kingdom proved his reverence for her.

Many historians hesitate to believe the Gāhaḍavālas of Kanauj to be a branch of Rāshṭrakūṭas. But in view of the reasons given to meet the various objections regarding this theory, which has been discussed in the first few chapters of this volume, it is evident that in fact the Gāhaḍavālas belonged to a branch of the Rāshṭrakūṭas and came to be so called because of their conquest of Gādhipur (Kanauj).

The history of the Rāshṭrakūṭas was first published in Hindi in my book named "Bhārata-kē-Prāchīna-Rāja Vamsha," Vol. III[2]. A synopsis of the first few chapters of this book, under the heading of "The Rāshṭrakūṭas and the Gāhaḍavālas" as well as its last chapter named "The Gāhaḍavālas of Kanauj" appeared in the Journal of the Royal Asiatic Society of Great Britain and Ireland, January 1930 and January 1932 respectively. The matter given in the appendix of this book was published in The "Indian Antiquary,"-

1 Indian Antiquary, Vol. XI, page 111.
2 Published in A. D. 1925.

January 1930. Hence, this volume is an attempt to bring out the history of the Rāshṭrakūṭas (Rāṭhōḍas) in a revised and enlarged form.

It will not be out of place here to express the gratitude to all those scholars whose efforts have been helpful in the preparation of this volume.

As the special letters "ṁ", and "ṅ", were not available, simple "m", and "n" have been used in their places and "sh" has been used for both श and ष. In some places simple "r" is used instead of "ṛ".

Archæological Department,
Jodhpur.

BISHESHWAR NATH REU,

CONTENTS.

THE RĀSHṬRAKŪṬAS.

In 269 B. C. (*i. e.*, 212 years before the Vikrama Era) there flourished a very powerful and religious king in India named Ashōka. He got his edicts inscribed on pillars set up in various provinces of his kingdom. In those found at Mānsērā, Shāhbāzgarhi (North-West Frontier Province), Girnār (Saurāshaṭra) and Dhavali (Kalinga) the words "Raṭhika," "Risṭika" (Rāshṭrika) or "Laṭhika" appear just after the mention of the Kāmbōjas and the Gāndhāras.

Dr. D. R. Bhandārkar, reading both the words "Rashṭika" (or Risṭika) and "Pētēnika" thus occurring as one, takes it to have been used to denote the hereditary governing families of Mahārāshṭra[1]. But, as the edict of Shāhbāzgarhi contains "यवन कंबोज गंधरनं रठिकनं पितिनिकनं" it appears that the words "Raṭhika" and "Pitinika" are used to denote two different tribes.[2]

Mr C V. Vaidya holds the word Rāshṭrika to denote the Rāshṭrakūṭas of the Mahārāshṭra[3] province, whom he considers to be the Mahāraṭṭa Kshatriyas[4], different from the Rāshṭrakūṭas of the north. But in the ancient books "Dīpavamsha" and "Mahāvamsha" of the Pālī language the word Mahāraṭṭa[5], and not Rāshṭrika, stands for the inhabitants of Mahārāshtra province.

---

1 Asōka by Bhanḍārkar, page 33. 2. In the "Anguttarnikāya" the words "[illegible]" and [illegible]" are also separately stated.

3 History of Mediaeval Hindu India, part II, page 323.

4 History of Mediaeval Hindu India, part II, pages 152-153.

5 From the cave inscriptions of Bhājā, Bēḍsā, Kārlī and Nānāghāṭ of the 2nd century of the Christian Era it appears that this Mahāraṭṭa tribe was very generous.

Dr. Hultzsch holds the words "Rathika" or "Raṭrika" (Rashṭrika) as pertaining to Ārāṭṭas of the Punjab. But if, in regard to the derivation of the word Āraṭṭa,[1] we were to apply the 'Bahuvrīhī Samāsa,' (आ समन्तात् व्याप्ता रट्टा यस्मिन् स आरट्टः) then the difference of opinion would be squared up to some extent. In the inscriptions of the Rāshṭrakūṭas a second name of their tribe is also found as "Raṭṭa". There should be no hesitation, therefore, in supposing that the Rāshṭrakūṭas were formerly the settlers of the Punjab, whence they migrated to the south and in the course of time carved out a kingdom in the Deccan.

A copper grant[2] of Rāshṭrakūṭa king Abhimanyu has been found from the Uṇḍikavāṭikā. As it bears no date, it is supposed to be of the beginning of the 7th century of V. S. It contains the words:-'ॐ स्वस्ति अनेकगुणगणालंकृतयशसां राष्ट्रकु(कू)[3]टाना (नां) तिलकभूतो मानांक इति राजा बभूव' i. e., king Mānānka, the greatest of the Rāshṭrakūṭa race, was adorned with virtue and fame.

---

1 Corpus Inscriptionum Indicarum, Vol. 1, page 56. In the "Mahābhārata" the "Araṭṭa" province is thus described:—

पंचनद्यो वहन्त्येता यत्र पीलुवनान्युत ॥ ३१ ॥
शतद्रुश्च विपाशा च तृतीरावती तथा ।
चन्द्रभागा वितस्ता च 'सिन्धुषष्ठ' बहिर्गिरः ॥ ३२ ॥
आरट्टा नाम ते देशाः..................

Karṇa Parva, Adhyāya-4,

i. e., the province irrigated by the waters of the Sutlej, the Bias, the Rāvī, the Chenāb, the Jhēlum, and the Indus and lying outside the mountains is called Āraṭṭa. At the time of the Mahābhārata this province was under the sway of king Shalya.

In the Dharma and Shraūta Sutras of Baudhāyana, this province is stated as a non-Āryan province (vide first prashna, first chapter and 18—12—13 respectively.)

In 326 B C. (269 years before Vikrama Era) the Āraṭṭas had opposed Alexander near Baluchistan as appears from the works of the contemporary writers.

2. Journal of the Bombay Asiatic Society, Vol. XVI, page 90.

3. Some people read कैकूटकानां in place of राष्ट्रकूटानां, but it is incorrect.

The stone inscription[1] of Rājā Dantidurga, fixed in the Dashāvatāra temple of the Ellora caves, contains the line:- 'न वेत्ति खलु कः क्षितौ प्रकटराष्ट्रकूटान्वयं' i. e., who is not aware of the world-famous Rāshṭrakūṭa race.

In a copper grant[2] of this very king dated Shaka Samvat 675 (V. S. 810 = A. D. 753) and also in that[3] of Nandarāja of Shaka S. 631 (V. S. 766 = A. D. 709) found at the village of Multai in the Central Provinces, the name of the dynasty is given as "Rāshṭrakūṭa". A similar name is found in inscriptions and grants of various other kings. But there are also some old writings, in which this clan is named as "Raṭṭa[4]" such as the inscription of Amōghavarsha I found at Sirūr, in which he is spoken of as" रट्टवंशोद्भव[5]

In a copper grant[6] of Indra III dated Shaka S. 836 (V. S. 971 = A. D. 914) found at Nausāri Amōghavarsha is described as the promoter of prosperity of the "Raṭṭa" race.

In the copper grant of Dēolī[7] it is stated that "Raṭṭa" was the originator of this dynasty and "Rāshṭrakūṭa" was his son from whom the dynasty took its name[8].

In an inscription of Ghōsūndi in Mewar the dynasty is named as "Rāshṭravarya" and in a copper grant of Nādōl[9] as "Rāshṭrauḍa."

1 Cave temples inscriptions, page 92. and Arch. Survey, Western India, Vol. V, page 87.

2 Indian Antiquary, Vol. XI, page 111.

3 Indian Antiquary, Vol. XVIII, page 234.

4 As "Māṭa", "Vaddiga" and "Chāpa" are the corrupt forms of "Mānyakhēṭa" Yādava Vishṇu Vardhna and "Chāpōtkaṭa" respectively, similarly "Raṭṭa" might also be a corrupt form of "Rāshṭrakūṭa".

5 Indian Antiquary, Vol. XII, page 218.

6 Journal Bombay Branch Royal Asiatic Society, Vol. XVIII, page 257.

7 Journal Bombay Branch Royal Asiatic Society, Vol. XVIII, pages 249-251. And Epigraphia Indica, Vol. V, page 192.

8 The birth of Rāshṭrakūṭa in the family of Raṭṭa is only a poetic conjecture.

9 Copper grant of Chauhāna Kīrtipāla of V. S. 1218.

In the word "Rāshṭrakūṭa" "Rāshṭra" means "kingdom" and "Kūṭa" denotes collection, "lofty" or "excellent". Thus, the word "Rāshṭrakūṭa" means" a great or excellent kingdom". The country ruled over by this dynasty might have been named "Mahārāshṭra[1]", which word is similarly formed by prefixing the syllable "Mahā" to the word "Rāshṭra".

In modern times, owing to the divergence of dialects, we come across many corrupt forms of the word "Rāshṭrakuṭa", such as, "Rāṭhavara, Rāṭhavaḍa, Rāṭhaura, Rāṭhauḍa[2], Rāṭhaḍa[3], Raṭhaḍā[4] and Rāṭhōḍa".

Dr. Burnely finding the word "Raṭṭa" used in the later writings of the Rāshṭrakūṭas[5] connects them with the Telugu-speaking 'Rēḍḍi' tribe. But the latter was a primitive tribe, while the Rāshṭrakūtas migrated to the south from the north. (This fact will be dealt with hereafter in a separate chapter). Therefore this theory is untenable.

In the court of Rājā Nārāyaṇa Shāha of Mayūragiri there flourished a poet named Rudra. By the order of the said king he compiled a poem named "Rāshṭrauḍha Vamsha Mahākāvya" in Shaka Samvat 1518 (V. S. 1653 =A. D. 1596), the first chapter of which contains the

1 Just as the country ruled over by the "Mālava" race was named Malwa, and that ruled over by the Gurjaras, Gujrat, similarly the country ruled over by the Rāshṭrakūṭas in Southern Kathiawar was named Saurāshṭra (Soraṭh) and the country between Narbada and Māhī named Rāṭ and "Lāṭ might be a corrupt form of it. (The country including the states of Alirajpur, Jhabua etc. is probably called Rāṭh.) In the inscription of Skandagupta on the Girnār hill, there is a mention of the "Sōraṭh" province. Thus, the names Rāshṭra (Rāṭh), Saurāshṭra (Sōrṭh) and Mahārāshṭra as applied to tracts bear testimony to the greatness of the Rāshṭrakūṭas.

2 This form is found in the inscription dated V. S. 1208, of Jasadhavala, found at Kōyalvāva (Godwar).

3 This form is mentioned in the inscription of Rāṭhora Salkhā, dated V. S. 1213, found at 'Vrihaspati Tank', 8 miles north-west of Jodhpur.

4 This form is found in the inscription of Rāō Sīhā of V. S. 1330, found at Bīṭhū (Dist. Pāli).

5 In the inscription of Rāṭhōḍa Hammīra of V. S. 1573, found at Phalodi, the word Rāshṭrakūṭa is used.

lines:- अलक्ष्यदेहा तमवोचदेषा राजन्नसावस्तु तवैकसूनुः। अनेन राष्ट्रं च कुलं तवोढं राष्ट्रौ (ष्ट्रो) ढनामा तदिह प्रतीतः॥ २६ ॥ i.e., (the Goddess Lātnā) thus addressed (Rājā-Nārāyaṇa) through the heavens, "He will be thy son and as he has maintained thy kingdom and family, his name will be "Rāshṭrōḍha".

EMIGRATION OF THE RĀSHṬRAKŪṬAS FROM THE NORTH TO THE SOUTH.

It has already been stated that Dr. Hultzsch holds[1] the Rāshṭrikas, mentioned in the edicts of Ashōka, and the Āraṭṭas, residing in the Punjab at the time of the Mahābhārata, to be of one and the same tribe. The Āraṭṭas existed in the Punjab up to the time of Alexander's invasion. Similarly, in the edicts of Ashōka of Mānsērā, Shāhbāzgarhi (N.W.F. Province), Girnār (Jūnāgadh) and Dhavalī (Kalinga), mention of the Rāshṭrika occurs just after the Kāmbōjas and the Gāndhāras. All these facts go to show clearly that the Rāshṭrakūṭas at first resided in the north-western[2] part of India and from there they afterwards migrated to the south. Dr. Fleet also holds the same opinion.

1. Corpus Inscriptionum Indicarum, Vol. I, page 56.

2. Though in some inscriptions of the Rāshṭrakūṭas they are stated to be 'Chandra Vamshīs', yet, in fact, they are 'Sūrya Vamshīs'. (This subject will be treated later in a separate chapter). The present rulers of Marwar consider themselves to be the descendants of Kusha, son of Rāmachandra of the Solar race. In the 'Vishṇu Purāṇa', 61 kings are named from Īkshvākū (a descendant of Sūrya), down to Shri Rāmachandra, and 60 names are enumerated from Shri Rāma to the last (Sūrya Vamshī) king Sumitra. Thus, from Īkshvākū down to Sumitra there are 121 names of kings in all (and 125 perhaps in the 'Bhāgavata'). Beyond this, there is no trace of the Solar kings in the Purāṇas. (According to the Purāṇas the time of Sumitra comes to about 3000 (?) years before this day.)

In the 'Uttar Kāṇḍa' of the 'Vālmīkīya Rāmāyaṇa,' Bharat, brother of Shri Rāmachandra, is stated to have conquered the Gandharvas (the people of *Kandhar*). It also informs us that Bharata had two sons, Taksha and Pushkala. Taksha founded the city of Takshashilā after his name, and Pushkala founded Pushkalāvata. Takshashilā is the modern Taxila. This city was situated in a circuit of 12 miles to the south-east of Hasanabdal and north west of Rawalpindi. Pushkalāvata was in the north-west near Peshawar. It is at present known as Chārsādā. Kusha, the son of Shri Rāmachandra, leaving Ayōdhyā, had founded the Kushāvatī city, near modern Mirzapur, on the bank of the Ganges. It is probable that owing to some mishap the

Mr. C. V. Vaidya holds the Rāshṭrakūṭas of the Deccan to be the Āryans of the south. But he presumes that they had settled there, having come from the north long before their establishing the kingdom in the Deccan for the second time. But, at the same time, he says that these Rāshṭrakūṭas were present in the Mahārāshṭra[1] even at the time of the edicts of Ashōka. The above conclusion of Mr. Vaidya is merely based on the situation of the edicts of Ashōka, which mention this clan. It has no sound basis, as two of such edicts were found in the North-West, one in Saurāshṭra and the other in Kalinga.

Dr. D. R. Bhanḍārkar, connecting the Rāshṭrakūṭās with the western provinces, holds them to be the residents of Mahārāshṭra.[2] But in the fifth edict of Ashōka, found at Shāhbāzgarhi it is thus stated:—

योन कंबोय गंधरनं रठिकनं पितिनिकनं येवपि अपरंत[3]

"Therefore it would be incorrect to connect the words 'रठिकनं पितिनिकनं with येवपि अपरंत.' The residents of the western provinces, mentioned here, might be some people different from the Rāshṭrakūṭas.

The family title of these Rāshṭrakūṭas was "Laṭalūrapurādhīshvara." Mr. Rajvade and others hold this Laṭalūrapura to be the modern Ratnapur in Bilaspur District (C.P.). If this supposition be correct, then the migration of the Rāṭhōras from the north to the south is proved.

---

descendants of Kusha might have gone up to their cousins, the descendants of Bharata, and in the course of time having acquired the name "Rāhsṭrika or Āraṭṭa" on their return had gone some to the north and others to the south *via* Girnār. But this is only imaginary.

We learn from the 'Rambhāmanjarī Nāṭikā' of Nayachandra Sūri that Jayachchandra was born in the Ikshvākū family (refer page 7.)

1. History of Mediaeval Hindu India, Part II, page 323.
2. Ashōka by D. R. Bhanḍārkar, page 33.
3. Corpus Inscriptionum Indicarum, Vol. I, page 55.

From the copper grant, dated Shaka S. 972 (V.S. 1107 = A.D. 1051), of the Sōlankī king Trilōchanapāla of Lāṭa we learn that Chālukya, the prime ancestor of the Sōlankīs had married the daughter of the Rāshṭrakūṭa king of Kanauj.[1] From this it is quite evident that the Rāshṭrakūṭās had also ruled over Kanauj[2] in the early period and about the sixth century of the Vikrama era they took possession of the kingdom of the Sōlankīs of the Deccan.

This fact is further proved by the copper grant of Sōlankī Rājarāja of the Deccan, issued in his 32nd regnal year (Shaka S. 975 = V. S. 1110 = A.D. 1053), found at Yēvūr, which informs that after king Udayana,[3] 59 kings of his dynasty ruled over Ayōdhyā. The last of these was Vijayāditya who founded the Sōlankī kingdom in the south. His 16 descendants ruled in the Deccan

---

1. समाविष्टार्थ संसिद्धौ तुष्टः स्रष्टाऽब्रवीच्च तम् ॥५॥
कान्यकुब्जे महाराज ! राष्ट्रकूटस्य कन्यकाम् ।
लब्ध्वा सुखाय तस्यां त्वं चौलुक्याप्नुहि संततिम् । ६ ।

(Indian Antiquary, Vol. XII, page 201)

2. Mr. J. W. Watson, Political Superintendent, Palanpur, writes that on Thursday Mangasira Sudi 5, Samvta 936 king Shrīpata Rāṭhōra of Kanauj, on accession to the Gaddi, had made a grant of 16 villages in the north of Gujrat to Chibadiā Brāhmaṇas, out of which village Ētā is still in the possession of their descendants.

Further, he writes that the ancient Arab Geographers have stated the boundary of Kanauj as being adjacent to Sindh. Almasudī has mentioned Sindh to be under the government of the king of Kanauj and the Mohmedan historians of Gujrat have also stated the king of Kanauj to be the master of Gujrat.

(Indian Antiquary, Vol. III, page 41.)

In quoting the writing of Mr. Watson here, we mean only to say that the Rāshṭrakūṭas were even formerly the kings of Kanauj and their kingdom extended far and wide. As regards Shrīpata we can only say that he perhaps being a member of the Kanauj royal family was called Kanaujēshvara. When king Dhruvarāja of Lāṭa had defeated the Pratihāra king Bhōjadēva of Kanauj he might have arranged for the grant of some districts of Kanauj to Shrīpata's father, who was a Rāshṭrakūṭa by caste. And afterwards Shrīpata on ascending the throne (on his father's death), might have made the aforesaid grant. The village Ētā is also described as having been granted by the Rāṭhoras of Kanauj in the Bombay Gazetteer, Vol. V, page 329.

3. In this grant Udayana is mentioned as 47th in descent from Brahmā.

after which their kingdom passed on to another dynasty. Here another dynasty means the Rāshṭrakūṭa dynasty, because it is stated in the copper grants of the Sōlankīs of Shaka S. 946 of Miraj and that of Shaka S. 999 of Yēvūr that Jayasimha, having defeated Rāshṭrakūṭa Indrarāja, again obtained the kingdom of the Chālukya dynasty.[1]

Kīrtivaraman, the great grandson of this Jayasimha, ascended the throne in V. S. 624. So his great grandfather Jayasimha may have lived about the second-half of the 6th century of the Vikrama era. Thus, it proves that the Rāshṭrakūṭās ruled here in the 6th century. Besides, it is also presumed that the marriage of the ancestor of the Sōlankīs with the daughter of the king of Kanauj might have taken place, when the former ruled at Ayōdhyā.

---

1. ....बभार

भूयश्चुलुक्यकुलवल्लभराजलक्ष्मीम् ।

(Indian Antiquary, Vol. VIII, Page 12.)

THE ORIGIN OF THE RĀSHṬRAKŪṬAS.

About 75 inscriptions and copper grants of the time of the Rāshṭrakūṭa kings of the Deccan and Gujarat have up to this time been found, in only 8[1] of which the Rāshṭrakūṭas are mentioned as belonging to the Yādava line.

The earliest of these containing the lineage of the Rāshṭrakūṭas, is of Shaka S. 782 (V. S. 917 = A.D. 860), while all the other inscriptions and copper plates of the earlier dates are silent on the point as to whether they are Sūrya Vamshīs or Chandra Vamshīs. Out of the

---

1 The 8 inscriptions and copper plates are as follows:—

The first of Shaka S. 782 (V. S. 917=A.D. 860) of king Amōghavarsha I, contains:—

तदीयभूपायत यादवान्वये.

(Epigraphia Indica, Vol. VI, page 29.)

The second of Shaka S. 836 (V. S. 971=A.D. 914) of Indrarāja III, contains:—

तस्माद्वंशो यदूनां जगति स ववृधे.

(Journal Bombay Asiatic Society, Vol. XVIII, page 261.)

The third of Shaka S. 852 (V. S. 987=A.D. 930) and the fourth of Shaka S. 855 (V. S. 990=A.D. 933) of Gōvindaraja IV, mention the lineage of the king as under:—

वंशो बभूव भुवि सिन्धुनिभो यदूनाम्

(Epigraphia Indica, Vol. VII, page 36 and Indian Antiquary, Vol. XII, page 249.)

The fifth of Shaka S. 862 (V. S. 997=A.D. 940) and the sixth of Shaka S. 880 (V. S. 1015=A.D. 958) of Krishnaraja III, state:—

यदुवंशे दुग्धसिन्धूपमाने

(Epigraphia Indica, Vol. V, page 192 and Vol. IV, page 281.)

The seventh of Shaka S. 894 (V. S. 1029=A.D. 972) is of Karkarāja II, which too contains:—

संमभूद्धन्यो यदोरन्वय:

(Indian Antiquary, Vol. XII, page 264.)

The eighth of Shaka S. 930 (V. S. 1065=A.D. 1008) is of Kakkala, which also bears:-

"सोऽपूर्वोस्तीह वंशो यदुकुलतिलको राष्ट्रकूटेश्वराणां"

(Epigraphia Indica, Vol. III, page 300.)

above 8, the copper grant of Shaka S. 836 goes a step further as follows:—

तत्रान्वये विततसात्यकिवंशजन्मा ।
श्रीदन्तिदुर्गनृपतिः पुरुषोत्तमोऽभूत् ॥

i.e., Rāshṭrakūṭa Dantidurga was born in the line of Yādava Sātyaki.[1]

But some time ago about 1800 silver coins of Rāshṭrakūṭa king Krishṇarāja I, were found at Dhamori (Amraoti). On the obverse of these, the head of the king is represented, while on the reverse there is a phrase as stated below:—

'परममाहेश्वर[2] महादित्यपादानुध्यात[3] श्री कृष्णराज'

This Krishṇarāja was ruling in V. S. 829 (A.D. 772) and it bears testimony to the fact that at that time the Rāshṭrakūṭas were considered to be of the Solar origin, and the followers of the 'Shaiva' religion.

A copper grant of Rāshṭrakūṭa Gōvindarāja III, dated Shaka S. 730 (V. S. 865 = A. D. 808) found at Rādhanpur contains:—

"यस्मिन् सर्वगुणाश्रये क्षितिपतौ श्रीराष्ट्रकूटान्वयो-
जाते यादववंशवन्मधुरिपावासीदलंघ्यः परैः ।"

i.e., by the birth of this virtuous king, the Rāshṭrakūṭa dynasty became as invincible as the Yādava dynasty by the birth of Shrī Krishṇa.

---

1 Halāyudha in his 'Kavirahasya' has also mentioned the Rāshṭrakūṭas as being the descendants of Yādava Sātyaki. Further, in the copper grant of Krishna III, dated Shaka S. 862 there is a similar description (तद्वंशजा जगति सात्यकिवंशभाजः).

2 In the copper grant of Gōvindachandra of V. S. 1174, the Gāhaḍavāla kings are also mentioned as 'Paramamāhēshvara' or staunch Shaivites.

3 The word 'पादानुध्यात' is generally preceded by the name of the father of the person mentioned after it. Here the 'महादित्य' alludes to the king's solar lineage, because in the documents hitherto discovered 'Mahāditya' appears neither as a title nor as a name of Krishṇarāja's father. Thus, it doubtlessly refers to his prime ancestor, the Sun.

From this it is quite evident that upto V.S. 865 (A.D. 808) the Rāshṭrakūṭa dynasty was considered as quite distinct from the Yādava family[1]. But later on, in the copper grant of Amōghavarsha I, dated Shaka S. 872, the Rāshṭrakūṭas are mentioned as the Yādavas. This is due to mistaking for identity the similitude of the Yādavas with the Rāshṭrakūṭas in the foregoing grant; and the authors of the subsequent 7 documents, without thinking over the matter, followed suit.

It may be objected why the Rāshṭrakūṭas did not care to rectify the mistake if, in fact, they did not belong to the Lunar stock. But instances of adherence to a mistaken theory adopted by the ancestors are not rare. The Sīsōdiyā family of the Māhāraṇās of Mēwār is considered, beyond any doubt, to be of the Solar origin, yet Rāṇā Kumbhā, one of the most talented rulers of this dynasty, following the opinions of his predecessors, describes in the 'Rasikapriyā,' a rendering by him on the 'Gītagōvinda' his prime ancestor Bāpā Rāvala, as the son of a Brāhmaṇa:—

'श्रीवैजवापेन सगोत्रवर्यः श्रीबप्पनामा द्विजपुंगवोऽभूत'

In the 'Rāshṭrauḍha Vamsha Mahākāvya' of V. S.

---

1 In the inscription of V. S. 1442 of the Yādava king Bhīma, found at Prabhāsapāṭan, it is thus stated:—

वंशो (शौ) प्रसिद्धो (द्धौ) हि यथा रवीन्दो (न्द्वोः)
राष्टोडवंशस्तु तथा तृतीयः ।
यत्राभवद्धर्मनृपोऽतिधर्म-
स्तस्माच्छिवं मा (सा) यमुना जगाम ॥१०॥

i.e., just as the two dynasties known as the Solar and the Lunar are famous, in the like manner, the third dynasty known as the Rāṭhōra is also famous. King Dharma of this dynasty married Yamunā, the daughter of king Bhīma.

('Sāhitya', Vol. I, part I, pages 279-281; and
Bombay Gazetteer, Vol. I, part II, pages 208-209.)

1653 (already mentioned), it is stated[1] that Goddess Lātanā brought the son, born of the Chandra (Moon), and handed him over to the Sūrya Vamshī king Nārāyaṇa of Kanauj, who had been observing penance for the birth of a son. And, as the child took upon himself the burden of the kingdom and the protection of the dynasty of the said Sūrya Vamshī king, he was named Rāshṭrōḍha. This shows that the Rāṭhōras, even at that time too, were considered to be Sūrya Vamshīs.

Similarly, in the inscriptions of the Gāhaḍavāla kings of Kanauj they have been mentioned as Sūrya Vamshīs :—

"आसीदर्शीतद्युतिवंशजातः क्ष्मापालमालासु दिवं गतासु ।
साक्षाद्विवस्वानिव भूरिधाम्ना नाम्ना यशोविग्रह इत्युदारः ॥

i.e., on the expiry of a line of kings, 'Sūrya Vamshī' Yashōvigraha, as powerful as the Sun himself, came to the throne.

These Gahāḍvāla Rāṭhōras were also Rāshṭrakūṭas, (this fact will be proved in the next chapter) therefore,

---

[1] पुरा कदाचिन्नतये समेतान्, देवाननुज्ञाप्य गृहाय सद्यः ।
कात्यायनीमर्धमृगाङ्कमौलिः, कैलासशैले रमयां बभूव ॥१२॥
....
अन्योन्य भूषापणबन्धरम्यं, तत्रान्तरे द्यूतमदीव्यतां तौ ॥१४॥
....
कात्यायनीपाणिसरोजकोश-विलोलिताक्षक्षपितादथेन्दोः ।
गर्भान्वितैकादशवार्षिकोऽभूदभूतपूर्वाप्रतिमः कुमारः ॥२०॥
....
तस्मै वरं साम्बशिवोदयालुः, श्रीकान्यकुब्जेश्वरतामदासीत् ॥२३॥
अत्रान्तरे काचन लातनाख्या, समेत्य देवी गिरिजाहराभ्याम् ।
विलीनभूमीपतिकान्यकुब्ज-राज्याधिपत्याय शिशुं ययाचे । २४ ।
....
नारायणो नाम नृपः सुतार्थी, यत्रेश्वरं ध्यायति सूर्यवंश्यः ॥
सा रुद्रदत्तेन सहामुनास्मिन्नवातरत् कांचनमेखलेन ॥२८॥
अलक्ष्यदेहा तमवोचदेषा, राजन्नसावस्तु तवैकसूनुः ॥
अनेन राष्ट्रं च कुलं तवोढं, राष्टौ (ष्ट्रो) ढनामा तदिह प्रतीतः ॥२९॥

the fact of the Rāshṭrakūṭas being 'Sūrya Vamshīs' is unquestionable.[1]

---

1 Though the earliest-known copper grant of the Rāshṭrakūṭa Abhimanyu contains no date, yet from its character it appears to be of about the beginning of the seventh century of the Vikrama era. The seal on it contains an image of a lion, the vehicle of Goddess Ambikā. Similarly, in the coins of Krishṇarāja I, he is described as 'Parama Māhēshvara' or a staunch Shaivite. But in the subsequent grants of the Rāshṭrakūṭas a 'Garuḍa' has been substituted for the lion. This shows that in the later period they might have been influenced by Vaishṇavism. (In view of the seals of these copper grants Bhagwan Lal Indraji has also formed a similar opinion—Journal of Bombay Asiatic Society, Vol. XVI, page 9.)

Therefore, like the Gōhila rulers of Bhaonagar, these kings also were considered to be 'Chandra Vamshīs' instead of 'Sūrya Vamshīs'. Formerly, when Gōhilas ruled over Kher (Mārwār), they were considered 'Sūrya Vamshīs. But after their migration to Kathiawar they came to be considered as 'Chandra Vamshīs' due to their being influenced by Vaishṇavism, as is evinced by the following stanza:—

'चन्द्रवंशि सरदार गोत्र गौतम वक्खाणुं
शाखा माधवि सार भके प्रवरत्रय जाणुं
अग्निदेव उद्धार देव चामुण्डा देवी
पांडव कुल परमाण माथ गोहिल चल एवी
विक्रमवधकरनारनृप शालिवाहन चकवै थयो
ते पछी तेज ओलादनो सोरठमां सेजक भयो ॥'

In the fifth edict of Ashōka, inscribed on the Girnār hill, there is a mention of the Rāshṭrakūṭas, and it shows that the latter had also some connection with that province.

THE RĀSHṬRAKŪṬAS
AND
THE GĀHAḌAVĀLAS.

As stated in a previous chapter, the Rāshṭrakūṭas originally migrated from the north to the south.

From the aforesaid copper grant, dated Shaka S. 972, of Sōlankī Trilōchanapāla, we learn that Chalukya, the prime ancestor of the Sōlankīs, had married the daughter of the Rāshṭrakūṭa king of Kanauj. Similarly, from the 'Rāshṭrauḍha Vamsha Mahākāvya' it is evident that the Rāshṭrakūṭas ruled at Kanauj at an earlier period.

An inscription[1] of Rāshṭrakūṭa king Lakhanapāla, who flourished[2] about V. S. 1258 (A .D. 1201), found at Badāūn, contains the following:—

प्रख्याताखिलराष्ट्रकूटकुलजक्ष्मापालदोः पालिता
पांचाला[3]भिधदेशभूषणकरी वोदामयूतापुरी ।
....
तत्रादितोऽभवदनन्तगुणो नरेन्द्र-
श्चन्द्रः स्वखड्गभयभीषितवैरिवृन्दः ।

i.e., the city of Badāūn, which is protected by the famous Rāshṭrakūṭa kings, is an ornament to the kingdom of Kanauj. Having overpowered the enemies with his strength, Chandra became its first king.

---

1 Epigraphia Indica, Vol. I, page 64.

2 Mr. Sanyal considers this inscription to be of a date prior to V. S. 1259 (A.D. 1202). This will be considered later on.

3 In the copper plate, dated V. S. 1150, of Chandradēva found at Badāūn the same word 'Panchāla' is used for Kanauj:—

चपलपंचालचूल-चुम्बन-चण-चन्द्रहासो ।
(Epigraphia Indica, Vol. XIV, page 193.)

A copper grant[1], dated V. S. 1148 (A.D. 1091), of Gāhaḍavāla Chandradēva found at Chandrāvatī (Benares District) contains:—

विध्वस्तोद्धतधीरयोधतिमिरः श्रीचन्द्रदेवो नृपः
येनोदारतरप्रतापशमिताशेषप्रजोपद्रवं
श्रीमद्गाधिपुराधिराज्यमसमं दोर्विक्रमेणार्जितम् ॥

i.e., Chandradēva, the son of Yashōvigraha, became a very powerful king in this dynasty. Having defeated his enemies by force of arms, he took the kingdom of Kanauj.

The dynasty of Chandradēva is not mentioned in this copper plate.

It is evident from both these documents that Chandradēva at first conquered Badāūn and afterwards took possession of Kanauj. The first of these documents belongs to those who designated themselves as 'Rāshṭrakūṭas,' and the second to those who later on assumed the title of 'Gāhaḍavāla.' But by taking into consideration the period of Chandradēva of the inscription and of the copper plate, it is found that Chandradēva, who had established his kingdom at Kanauj and Chandradēva, from whom the Badāūn line took its origin, was one and the same person. His eldest son Madanapāla became king of Kanauj, and the younger son Vigrahapāla[2] got Badāūn as 'Jāgīr.' The members of the Badāūn family continued to be called 'Rāshṭrakūṭas' but those of the Kanauj family, in the course of time, came to be known as Gāhaḍavālas[3] after Gādhipura (Kanauj). This changed

1 Epigraphia Indica, Vol. IX, pages 302-305.

2 Perhaps Chanda Bardāī, the author of the 'Rāsō,' has also mentioned Lakhanapāla, the descendant of this Vigrahapāla of Badāūn, as a nephew of Jayachandra.

3 The word "Gāhaḍa" in the "Ḍingala" language means "firmness" and "power." Therefore, when the kings of this dynasty became powerful and strong, it is probable that, they might have assumed this title, or just as the Rāshṭrakūṭas of the village Rainka (in U.P.) have come to be called Rainkvāls; in the like manner the Rāshṭrakūṭas of this branch, being the residents or rulers of Gādhipura (Kanauj), were styled as Gāhaḍavālas. For in the corrupt "Prākrita"

name of the dynasty appears in only the copper grants of V. S. 1161, 1162 and 1166 of the prince regent Gōvindachandra[1] as well as in the inscription of his queen Kumāradevī.[2]

By taking these facts into consideration we conclude that at first the Rāshṭrakūṭas held sway over Kanauj, after whom the Guptas, the Baisas, the Maukharīs and the Pratihāras[3] ruled there one after another. But from the copper grant[4] of Shaka Samvat 836 (V. S. 971), issued by the Rāshṭrakūṭa king Indrarāja III, it appears that he in his invasion of the North, having conquered Upēndra, had laid waste Mērū (Kanauj). Probably, Pratihāra Mahīpāla was then ruling there.

After this invasion, the kingdom of the Pratihāras (Paḍihāras) became weak and their feudatories began to declare independence.[5] From this it appears that about V. S. 1111 (A.D. 1054) Chandra of the Rāshṭra-

---

language the form of Gādhipura might have become "Gāhaḍa" instead of "Gāhi-ur." It may also be noted that when Rāo Sīhā severed all his connections with Kanauj and migrated to Mārwār, he abandoned his surname Gāhaḍavāla and acknowledged himself as simple Rāshṭrakūṭa.

1 वंशे गाहडवालाख्ये बभूव विजयी नृपः

2 Epigraphia Indica, Vol. IX, P. 324.

3 In V. S. 924 (A.D. 867) the Rāshṭrakūṭa king Dhruvarāja II of "Lāṭa" (Gujrat) had defeated Pratihāra king Bhōjadēva of Kanauj. It was Nāgabhata II, the grandfather of this Bhōjadēva, who probably established his capital at Kanauj by defeating Rāshṭrakūṭa Chakrāyudha, the successor of Indrāyudha.

History of Rājpūtāna, Vol. I, page 161, footnote 1.

4 कृतगोवर्धनोद्धारं हेलोन्मूलितमेरुणा ।
उपेन्द्रमिन्द्रराजेन जित्वा येन न विस्मितम् ॥

Journal Bombay Asiatic Society, Vol. XVIII, page 261. This fact is also borne out by the copper grant, dated Shaka Samvat 852, of Gōvinda IV, in which it is stated that Indrarāja III, with his horsemen, crossed the Jamuna and laid waste the city of Kanauj:—

तीर्णा यत्तुरगैरगाधयमुना सिन्धुप्रतिस्पर्द्धिनी
येनेदं हि महोदयारिनगरं निर्मूलमुन्मूलितम् ।

5 Even before this, between V. S. 842 and 850 (A.D. 785 and 793), the kingdom of Dhruvarāja had extended up to Ayōdhyā in the north. Later, between V. S. 932 and 971 (A.D. 875 and 914), in the time of Krishṇarāja II, it spread up to the banks of the Ganges and between V. S. 997 and 1023 (A.D. 940 and 966), in the time of Krishṇarāja III, it had extended further north crossing the Ganges.

kūṭa family, taking possession of Badāūn, might have afterwards conquered Kanauj. After the death of this Chandra his eldest son might have succeeded him at Kanauj and Badāūn might have been given in his life-time, as a 'Jāgīr' to his second son.

Later, when Harishchandra, the son of Jayachchandra, lost his kingdom of Kanauj, his descendants settled at Mahui in the district of Farrukhabad. But, when the Mohammedans took possession of these places also, Sīhāji, the grandson of Jayachchandra, (son of Baradāisēna) left the country for pilgrimage and reached Mārwār. Here his descendants rule even to this day and consider themselves to be the descendants of Rāshṭrakūṭa king Jayachchandra.

There still exist ruins at Mahui which are locally known as 'Sīhā Rāo-kā-Khēḍā.'

Rāo Jōdhā, a descendant of Rāo Sīhā, built the fort and founded the town of Jodhpur in V. S. 1516 (A.D. 1459). From the contents of a copper grant, issued by him, it appears that in the time of Rāo Dhūhaḍa, grandson of Rāo Sīhā, a Sārasvata Brāhmaṇa named Lumba ṛishi brought down from Kanauj the idol of 'Chakrēshvarī', the family deity of the Rāṭhōras, which was then installed at the village of Nāgāṇā.

In some old manuscript chronicles this idol is said to have been brought from Kalyāṇī.[1] But this Kalyāṇī too must be the Kalyāṇa-Kaṭaka (cantonment) of Kanauj.

All these facts go to prove that the Rāshṭrakūṭas and the Gāhaḍavālas are one and the same.

Dr. Hoernle considers the Gāhaḍavāla family to be a branch of the Pāla dynasty. He is of opinion that the descendants of Nayapāla, the eldest son of Mahīpāla, ruled over the province of Gauḍa (Bengal) and that Mahīpāla's younger son, Chandradēva, took the

---

1 Some people think that it was Kōnkan of the Deccan. But in the face of the proofs adduced above, the supposition does not seem to be correct.

kingdom of Kanauj. But this does not seem to be correct. Because firstly, neither in the inscriptions of the Pāla kings are they mentioned as Gāhaḍavālas, nor is there any mention of the Pāla dynasty in the inscriptions of the Gāhaḍavālas. Secondly, the ending 'Pāla' occurs in the name of all the kings of the Pāla dynasty from its founder Gōpāla I, to its last king ; whereas, only one, out of the 8 Gāhaḍavāla kings, has used the suffix Pāla in his name. Thirdly, the mere fact of a word being found in the names of two persons, should not be regarded as evidence of the two persons being identical. The names of the kings of the two dynasties are given below:—

Pāla dynasty.		Gāhaḍavāla dynasty.
Vigrahapāla	.. ..	Yashōvigraha.
|		|
Mahīpāla	.. ..	Mahīchandra.
|		|
Nayapāla	.. ..	Chandradēva.

The word 'Vigraha' is common to the names Vigrahapāla and Yashōvigraha. Similarly, the word 'Mahī' is found in the names Mahīpala and Mahīchandra. We know that Mahipāla of the Pāla dynasty was a powerful king who had regained the lost kingdom of his father and constructed many temples in Benares, through his sons (?) Sthirapāla and Vasantapāla, while Mahīchandra of Gāhaḍavāla dynasty was not even an independent ruler. Hence, such coincidence by itself can in no way be supposed to prove that Mahipāla and Mahīchandra were one and the same person.[1]

Fourthly, the dates of the inscriptions of the kings of the Pāla dynasty are indicated by their regnal

1 Moreover, there is an interval of 65 years between the issue of the copper grant of Pāla king Māhīpāla dated V. S. 1083 (A.D 1026) and that of Gāhaḍavāla Chandradēva of V. S. 1148 (A.D. 1091), which produces doubt as to whether these two kings were father and son. The last copper grant of Chandradēva hitherto discovered is of V. S. 1156 (A.D. 1099).

years[1] instead of by the Vikrama Samvat; whereas the grants of the Gāhaḍavāla kings bear Vikrama Samvat and not the regnal years. Fifthly,[2] kings Dharmapāla and Rāyapāla of the Pāla dynasty had married the daughters of the Rāshṭarkūṭa kings Parabala and Tunga respectively; and it has, ere this, been established by proofs that the Rāshṭrakūṭas and the Gāhaḍavālas are collaterals. Therefore, Dr. Hoernle's supposition is not reasonable.

Mr. Vincent Smith considers the northern Rāshṭrakūṭas (Rāṭhōras) to be the off-shoots of the Gāhaḍavālas and the Rāshṭrakūṭas of Deccan to be the descendants of the non-Āryans.[3] But in the light of the above facts this supposition also seems groundless. Moreover, their marrying the daughters of the Sōlankīs and the Yādavas proves them to be pure Kshatriyas.

Kāshmīrī Pandit Kalhaṇa in his well-known history of Kāshmīr, named 'Rājataranginī', written in the twelfth century of the Vikrama era, mentions 36 clans of the Kshatriyas[4]. In Vikrama S. 1422, Jayasimha had commenced writing the 'Kumārapāla charita' in which he has enumerated the 36 clans mentioning only "Raṭṭa" as one of them but there is no mention of the Gāhaḍavālas. Similarly, in the 'Prithvīrāja Rāsō' the name Rāṭhōra alone occurs but not Gāhaḍavāla. Further, Jayachandra is also stated in it as being a Rāṭhōra.

The Rājā of Rāmpur (Farrukhabad district), the Rāo of Khimsēpur (Mainpuri district) and the chaudharīs of Surjā and Sorḍā, allege themselves to be Rāṭhōras, descended from Jajpāla, the son of

1 Among the inscriptions of the Pāla kings, there is only one of Mahīpāla that bears a Vikrama Samvat (1083).

2 This custom was not strictly observed (See p. 32.)

3 Early History of India, (1924), pages 429-430.

4 प्रख्यापयन्तः संभूतिं षट्त्रिंशति कुलेषु ये ।
तेजस्विनो भास्वतोपि सहन्ते नोष्णकैः स्थितिम् ॥ १६१७॥
Rājataranginī, Taranga VII.

Jayachchandra. Similarly, the Rājās of Bijaipur and Māṇḍā think themselves to be the descendants of Māṇika Chandra, the brother of Jayachchandra, and are called Chandravamshī Gāhaḍavāla Rāṭhōras.[1] From this, too, we conclude that the "Gāhaḍavāla" was the name of a branch of the Rāshṭrakūṭa dynasty.

In the face of so many strong proofs it would be unreasonable to think that the Gāhaḍavālas and the Rāshṭrakūṭas are of different origins.

Mr. N. B. Sanyāl thinks[2] that, as the title 'Gādhipurādhipa' (master of Kanauj) is attached to the name of Gōpāla in the Budhist inscription[3] of V. S. 1176 (A.D. 1118), found at Sēṭ Māhēṭh, the Gōpāla and his successor Madanpāla mentioned in it are identical with the Gōpāla and the Madanapāla of the inscription of Rāshṭrakūṭa king Lakhanapāla of Badāūn. Gōpāla had taken possession of Kanauj in the last quarter of the eleventh century A.D. *i.e.*, some time between the overthrow of the Pratihāra dynasty of Kanauj in V. S. 1077 (A.D. 1020) and the establishment of Gāhaḍavāla kingdom of Kanauj by Chandradēva towards the close of the 11th century A.D. And this Chandra had seized the kingdom of Kanauj from the very Gōpāla. This is the reason why the title Gādhipurādhipa appears with the name of Gōpāla alone in the Sēṭ Māhēṭh inscription.

Further, Mr. Sanyāl proceeds to quote the following couplet from the copper grant[4] of Shaka S. 972 (V. S. 1107=A.D. 1050) of Sōlankī Trilōchanapāla discovered at Surat.

कान्यकुब्जे महाराज राष्ट्रकूटस्य कन्यकाम् ।
लब्ध्वा सुखाय तस्यां त्वं चालुक्याप्नुहि सन्ततिम् ॥

1 People of Shamsābād say that after the fall of Kanauj some of the descendants of Jayachchandra had gone to Nēpāl and they called themselves Rāṭhōras. Some fifty years ago on auspicious occasions such as marriage, etc., they used to send for a brick from Shamsābād. This indicates their love for their motherland.

2 Journal Bengal Asiatic Society, (1925), Vol. XXI, page 103.

3 Indian Antiquary, Vol. XXIV, page 176.

4 Indian Antiquary, Vol. XII, page 201.

This testifies the rule of the Rāshṭrakūṭas over Kanauj at an early period.

Mr. Sanyāl then cites the aforesaid Sēṭh Māhēṭh inscription as a proof of the above.

Let us examine this theory critically.

From the copper grant[1] of V. S. 1084 (A.D. 1027) of Pratihāra Trilōchanapāla, and from the inscription[2] of V.S. 1093 (A.D. 1036) of Yashahpāla, we understand that the rule of the Pratihāras' over Kanauj had probably continued even after this date. In the copper grant[3] of V.S. 1148 (A.D. 1091) of Gāhaḍavāla king Chandra it is thus stated:—

तीर्थानि काशिकुशिकोत्तरकोशलेन्द्र-
स्थानीयकानिपरिपालयताऽभिगम्य ।
हेमात्मतुल्यमनिशं ददता द्विजेभ्यो-
येनाङ्किता वसुमती शतशस्तुलाभिः ॥

This shows that long before the writing of this copper grant, king Chandra had taken possession of Kanauj. For, there is in the above stanza a reference to his several charitable grants of gold weighing as much as his person after a mention of his conquests of Kāshī, Kushika and north Kōshala.

He must have taken some years in performing such great deeds. Therefore, the supposition that Chandra had conquered Kanauj in the last part of the 11th century A.D. and that before this, *i.e.*, in the last quarter of the same century Kanauj was ruled over by Gōpāla of the Rāshṭrakūṭa dynasty of Badāūn, does not appeal much to reason.

Further, in ascertaining the date of Lakhanapāla's inscription[4], Mr. Sanyāl says that Qutubuddīn Aibak,

1 Indian Antiquary, Vol. XVIII, page 34.
2 Journal Bengal Asiatic Society, Vol. V, page 731.
3 Epigraphia Indica, Vol. IX, page 304.
4 Epigraphia Indica, Vol. I, page 64.

conquering Badāūn in A.D. 1202 (V. S. 1259), granted that territory as 'Jāgīr' to Shamsuddīn[1] Altamash. This inscription of Lakhanapāla must, therefore, be of a date just before V.S. 1259. According to this opinion if we take Lakhanapāla's inscription to be of V.S. 1258, *i.e.*, a year before this date, there occurs a period of 82 years between this and the Budhist inscription, dated V.S. 1176 (A.D. 1118), of king Madanapāla found at Sēṭ Māhēṭh. And this period is quite reasonable for the four generations that intervened between Madanapāla and Lakhanapāla. Again, by supposing V. S. 1171 (A.D. 1114) as the date of the Mohammedan invasion (in which according to Mr. Sanyāl, Madanapāla had fought in the capacity of a feudatory of the Gāhaḍavāla king Gōvindachandra of Kanauj), which is mentioned in the Budhist inscription[2] of Kumārdēvī, the queen of king Gōvindachandra, and by counting back 60 years from this date for the reigns of the 3 ancestors of Madanapāla of Badāūn, the time of his fourth ancestor *i.e.*, king Chandradēva comes to about V. S. 1111 (A.D. 1054). Under the circumstances, if the date of the birth of king Chandra be supposed to be about V. S. 1090 (A.D. 1033) his having lived to an age of 67 years upto V. S. 1157 (A.D. 1100) is not an impossibility. His long life is also proved by the fact that in V. S. 1154 (A.D. 1097), in all probability due to old age, he had in his life-time, transferred the reins of the government to his son Madanapāla of Kanauj. And only three years afterwards, in V. S. 1157 (A.D. 1100) when he died, even his son Madana had grown old. He, too, made over the government of his kingdom to his son Gōvindachandra in V. S. 1161 (A. D. 1104) and died in V. S. 1167 (A.D. 1110).

1 Elliot's History of India, Vol. II, page 232 and 'Tabqāt-i-Nāsiri' (Raverty's translation), page 530.

2 Epigraphia Indica, Vol. IX, page 324.

The death of Chandra is held to have occurred in V. S. 1157 (A.D. 1100). From this we conclude that Vigrahapāla (who being his younger son, was given the 'Jāgīr' of Badāūn) and his son Bhuvanpāla of the Badāūn inscription might have died during Chandra's life-time and that Gōpāla ruled over Badāūn at the time of Chandra's death. It is also probable that his younger son Vigrahapāla and the latter's son Bhuvanpāla, having predeceased, Chandra in V. S. 1154 (A.D. 1097), being disgusted with the worldly affairs, might have renounced the kingdom and raised his eldest son Madanapāla to the throne of Kanauj. Chandra's existence might account for the intimate relations that existed between the two families of Kanauj and Badāūn upto the time of Gōpāla. Due to this fact, or that of the late birth of the heir-apparent Gōvindachandra and the probability of Gōpāla's being taken in adoption, or for some other reason the title 'Gādhipurādhipa' might have been attached to the name of Gōpāla. But in the time of his (Gōpāla's) son due to the disappearance of such causes and also due to the establishment of the relation of a monarch and a feudatory between the two families, the title ceased to apply to Madanapāla. In course of time it might have been thought improper to use this title with the name of Gōpāla even. Had Gōpāla, in fact, conquered Kanauj, the title 'Gādhipurādhipa' must have also been mentioned with his name in the Badāūn inscription.

It does not appear reasonable that the writer of the Badāūn inscription, who exults in making such a high sounding mention (यत्पौरुषात्प्रवरतः सुरसिन्धुतीरहम्मीरसंगमकथा न कदाचिदासीत *i. e.,* owing to the valour of Madanapāla the Mohammedans did not ever dream of coming near the banks of the Ganges) of the battle fought by the ancestor of his patron in the capacity of a feudatory only, should have forgotten to take notice of such a remarkable deed as the conquest of Kanauj by Madan's father, Gōpāl.

Taking all these facts into consideration if we suppose the two Chandras, *viz.*, that of Badāūn and the conqueror of Kanauj, as one and the same, most of the controversies disappear; and there appears no objection to doing so.

The Rāshṭrakūṭa family of Kanauj mentioned in the copper plate of V. S. 1107 (A.D. 1050) of Sōlankī Trilōchanapāla, refers only to the Rāshṭrakūṭa family contemporary with the prime ancestor of the Chālukya clan, who is said to have married in it and not the later one. The inscription of Sēṭ Māhēṭh, therefore, cannot be of much importance to support that theory.

OTHER OBJECTIONS.

In this chapter some more objections to the theory of the Rāshṭrakūṭas and the Gāhaḍavālas being the members of one and the same dynasty will be considered:—

Historians of the East and the West, who hesitate to admit the Rāshṭrakūṭas of the Deccan and the Gāhaḍavālas of Kanauj to be of one and the same dynasty, offer the following reasons for their doubts.

(1) That in the inscriptions of the Rāshṭrakūṭas they are stated as of the Lunar dynasty, while the Gāhaḍavālas assert that they belong to the Solar stock.

(2) That the 'gōtra' of the Rāshṭrakūṭas is 'Gautama', while that of the Gāhaḍavālas is 'Kāshyapa.'

(3) That in the copper grants of the Gāhaḍavālas they are not stated as "Rāshṭrakūṭas" but only as "Gāhaḍavālas."

(4) That the Rāshṭrakūṭas and the Gāhaḍavālas used to intermarry.

(5) That the other 'Kshatriyas' do not consider the Gāhaḍavālas to be of a high and pure descent.

(1) In a previous chapter named "The Origin of the Rāshṭrakūṭas" we have already discussed this subject. But leaving aside those facts, it may be stated that the classification of dynasties as the Solar, the Lunar, and the Fire dynasties was made only in the 'Paurāṇik' age; for the kings of the same dynasty are in some inscriptions stated as belonging to the Solar stock, while in others to the Lunar or Fire dynasty. Here we quote some instances for reference.

The family of the Mahārāṇās of Udaipur (Mewar) is well-known in India to be of the Solar origin; but in the inscription dated V.S. 1331 (A.D. 1274) of Chitorgarh it is stated to be as follows:—

जीयादानन्दपूर्वं तदिह पुरमिलाखंडसौन्दर्यशोभि-
क्षोण्यीप्र (पृ) ष्ठस्थमेव त्रिदशपुरमधः कुर्व्वदुच्चैः समृद्धया
यस्मादागत्य विप्रश्चतुरुदधिमहीवेदिनिक्षिप्तयूपो-
बप्पाख्यो वीतरागश्चरणयुगमुपासीत हारीतराशेः ।

i.e., Bappa (the prime ancestor of the Mahārāṇās), a Brāhmaṇa, coming from Ānandapur, worshipped the sage Hārīta.

This fact is also proved by the inscription, of Samarsimha, dated V. S. 1342 (A.D. 1285) and found in the monastery near Achalēshvara temple at Abu.

The book named 'Ēklinga Māhātmya', compiled in the time of Rāṇā Kumbhā, states:—

आनन्दपुरविनिर्गत विप्रकुलानन्दनो महीदेवः ।
जयति श्रीगुहदत्तः प्रभवः श्रीगुहिलवंशस्य ॥

i.e., Guhadatta, a Brāhmaṇa coming from Ānandapur, founded the 'Guhila' dynasty.

In the beginning of the 'Rasikapriyā', a commentary by Rāṇā Kumbhā himself, on the "Gīta Gōvinda" of Jayadēva, it is stated:—

श्रीवैजवापेन सगोत्रवर्यः श्रीबप्पनामा द्विजपुंगवोऽभूत् ।
हरप्रसादादपसादराज्यप्राज्योपभोगाय नृपोऽभवद्यः ॥

i.e., Bappa, a Brāhmaṇa, of the 'Vaijavāpa Gōtra,' got a state by the favour of "Shiva."

In the inscription of Guhilōta Bālāditya, found at Chātsū in the Jaipur State, it is stated:—

ब्रह्मक्षत्रान्वितोऽस्मिन्समभवदनमे............

i.e., combining in himself the powers of a warrior and of a priest (like Parashurāma), Bhartṛibhaṭṭa became a king in this dynasty. (The poet here has very nicely expressed himself by using the word "ब्रह्मक्षत्र").

From the above references one can easily presume that the founder of the famous Guhilōta dynasty of Mewar was a Nāgara Brāhmaṇa of the 'Vaijavāpa Gōtra.' But are the historians prepared to accept this theory ?

Similar is the case of the Sōlankī (Chālukya) dynasty. In the inscription, of Sōlankī Vikramāditya VI, dated V. S. 1133 (A.D. 1076), it is stated as follows:—

> ओं स्वस्तिसमस्तजगत्प्रसूतेर्भगवतो
> ब्रह्मणः पुत्रस्यात्रेर्नेत्रसमुत्पन्नस्य यामिनी-
> कामिनीललामभूतस्य सोमस्यान्वये × × ×
> श्रीमानस्ति चालुक्यवंशः ।

i.e., the Chālukya dynasty traces its origin to the Moon. This fact is also established by their other inscriptions, by the 'Dvyāshraya Kāvya' of Hēmachandra, and by 'Vastupālacharita' of Jinaharshagaṇi.

In the copper grant, dated V. S. 1200 (A.D. 1143), of Kulōttungachūḍadēva II, the Chālukyas are said to be Chandravamshīs, belonging to 'Mānavya Gōtra', and the descendants of the sage Hārīti.

Bilhaṇa, the well-known Kashmīrī poet, in his "Vikramānkadēva Charita", has stated the descent of this (Chālukya) dynasty from the handful of water by Brahmā. The same fact is proved by the inscription, dated V. S. 1208 (A.D. 1151), of the time of Sōlankī Kumārapāla, by the Kanthunātha inscription of Khambhāt, and by the copper grant, dated V.S. 1107 (A.D. 1050), of Trilōchanapāla.

In the inscription of Bilhārī (Jabalpur district), of the time of Yuvarājadēva II of the Haihaya (Kalachuri) dynasty the Chālukya dynasty is stated to have originated from the handful of water of Drōṇa[1]; but in the 'Prithvīrāja Rāsō' the Sōlankīs are stated to be 'Agni vamshīs.'

At present, the Sōlankīs (and the Baghēlas)[2] themselves admit that their originator Chālukya had sprung from the sacrificial fire of Vashishṭha.

---

1 Epigraphia Indica, Vol. I, page 257.

2 A branch of the Sōlankīs.

Now, let us consider the origin of Chauhānas.

In the inscription, dated V. S. 1225 (A.D. 1168), discovered by Col. James Tod in the Hānsī Fort, and in that of V.S. 1377 (A.D. 1320) of Dēvaḍā (Chauhāna) Rāo Lumbhā, found at the Achalēshvara temple at Abu, the Chauhānas are said to belong to the Lunar dynasty, and to 'Vatsa Gōtra; while in the inscriptions of the time of Vīsaladēva IV, in the 'Hammīra Mahākāvya' of Nayachandra Sūri, and in the 'Prithvīrājavijya Mahākāvya' the Chauhānas are said to belong to the Solar dynasty. Contrary to both these opinions, the 'Prithvīrāja Rāsō,' and the Chauhānas of the present day hold that their originator had sprung from the sacrificial fire of the sage Vashishṭha.

The origin of the Paramāra dynasty stands as below:—

In the 'Navasāhasānka Charita,' written by Padmagupta (Parimala), the originator of this dynasty is said to have sprung from the sacrificial fire of Vashishṭha; and in their inscriptions as well as in "Tilaka Manjarī", written by Dhanapāla, the same opinion is upheld. But Halāyudha, in his "Pingala Sūtra Vṛitti", has quoted a verse in which king Munja of the Paramāra dynasty is said to have been born of the priest-warrior stock (ब्रह्मक्षत्रकुलीन), which is worth consideration.

Further, the modern Paramāra rulers of Malwa allege themselves to be the descendants of the famous king Vikramāditya. But from the documents of their ancestors this allegation finds no support.

Similarly, views about the origin of the Pratihāra (Paḍihāra) dynasty are also different. Some think this dynasty to have originated[1] from a Brahmaṇa named Harishchandra and a Kshatriyā lady named Bhadrā;

[1] विप्रः श्रीहरिचन्द्राख्यः पत्नी भद्रा च क्षत्रिया ।
ताभ्यान्तु [ये सुता] जाताः [प्रतिहा]रांश्च तान्विदुः ॥५॥
Inscription, dated V. S. 940, of Pratihāra Bāuka.

while others say that the originator of this dynasty had sprung from the sacrificial fire of Vashishṭha.

Looking to these controversies, we should not be surprised to see the misrepresentation about the dynasty of the Rāshṭrakūṭas. Perhaps, all this confusion regarding the origin of the different dynasties has arisen from the belief in the legends of the Purāṇas. Hence, this belief should have no importance from the historical point of view.[1]

(2) Vigyānēshvara says that the 'Gōtras' and the 'Pravaras' of the Kshatriyas accord with those of their priests[2]. Therefore, it appears that the above theory was prevalent upto the 12th century of the Vikrama era. It is probable that when the Rāshṭrakūṭas came to Kanauj, their old priests might have been left behind and new ones appointed, which brought about the change of their 'Gōtra' from 'Gautama' to 'Kāshyapa.' It is also possible that this 'Gautama Gōtra' might have been assumed by them on their coming to Marwar, before which they belonged to the 'Kāshyapa Gōtra.'

In the inscriptions of the ruling families, the mention of these 'Gōtras' is very rare. Hence, it is also possible that, in the course of time, having forgotten their original 'Gōtra,' they might have adopted the 'Kāshyapa Gōtra' as is usual in such cases. Under the circumstances, it does not seem proper to consider the

1 In the inscription of the Kalachuri Vijjala of the southern India, dated Shaka S. 1084, the Rāsṭrakūṭas are stated, out of malice, as belonging to the 'Daitya vamsha'. (Epigraphia Indica, Vol. V, page 16).

2 राजन्यविशां······पुरोहितगोत्रप्रवरौ वेदितव्यौ
(पौरोहित्यान् राजन्यविशां प्रवृणीते–इत्याह आश्वलायन;)
याज्ञवल्क्यस्मृति. विवाहप्रकरण–असमानार्षगोत्रजां–
Commentary on verse 53.

This fact is also proved by the following stanza quoted from the Ashvaghōsha's 'Saundarānada Mahākāvya', composed in the second century of the Vikrama era.

गुरोर्गोत्रादत: कौत्सास्ते भवन्ति स्म गौतमा: ॥२२॥
Saundarānand Mahākāvya, [illegible]]

Rāshṭrakūṭas and the Gāhaḍvālas, who have been held as collaterals for ages, to be of different lineages, merely on account of the difference of their 'Gōtras.'

(3) An inscription of Pratihāra Bāuka, found at Jodhpur, contains.

भट्टिकं देवराजोऽयं वल्लमण्डलपालकम् ।
निपात्य तत्क्षणं भूमौ प्राप्तवान् छत्रचिह्नकम् ॥

i.e., who obtained the Umbrella after killing the Bhāṭī king Dēvarāja of the 'Valla Manḍala.'

Again :—

[भट्टि] वंश विशुद्धायां तदस्मात् कक्कभूपतेः ।
श्रीपद्मिन्यां महाराज्ञ्यां जातः श्रीबाउकः सुतः ॥२६॥

i.e., a son named Bāuka was born to king Kakka from his wife of the Bhāṭī clan.

In these inscriptions the writer has omitted the name of the famous Yādava clan, and has only mentioned its Bhāṭī branch. Are we to infer from this that the Bhāṭīs are of a different lineage from the Yādavas? If not, on what good grounds are we to suppose the Rāshṭrakūṭas and the Gāhaḍavālas as being of different origins ? Can we arrive at such a conclusion from the mere fact that in only the three copper grants of the prince regent, Gōvindachandra, of V. S. 1161, 1162 and 1166, as well as in the inscription of his queen Kumāradēvī no mention is made of the Rāshṭrakūṭa dynasty, but of its Gāhaḍavāla branch.[1]

---

1 In the inscription of the Chandēla Kshatriyas they are mentioned as Chandrātrēyas, that is, the descendants of Chandra, the son of Atri.

In the 'Prithvīrāja Rāsō,' their origin is stated to be from the Moon and Hēmavatī, the widowed daughter of Hēmarāja, the priest of the Gāhaḍavāla king Indrajit; but the Chandēlas allege that they are the collaterals of the Rāshṭrakūṭas. They had ruled over Bundēlkhand and its neighbouring places.

Similarly, the Bundēlas are also held to be the collaterals of the Gāhaḍavālas? (Some Paramāras, Chauhānas, etc., also have subsequently got mixed in these Bundēlas?). At present the rulers of Ōrchhā, Tehrī, Pannā, etc., are of the Bundēla clan

Even at the present day the Rājpūtas belonging to the Dēvaḍā or Sīsōdiya branches of the Chauhāna[1] or Guhilōta clans respectively, when asked, do not declare themselves as Chauhānas or Guhilōtas but simply say that they are Dēvaḍās or Sīsōdiyās. Further, the era founded by the famous Haihaya clan is named after their branch as 'Kalachuri Samvat' and 'not Haihaya Samvat.'

(4) An inscription of queen Kumāradēvī of Mahārājādhirāja Govindachandra has been found at Sāranātha[2] from which we learn that she was the grand-daughter (daughter's daughter) of Mahaṇa, the Rāshṭrakūṭa. In the 'Rāmacharita', compiled by Sandhyākaranandī, this Mahaṇa (Mathana) is said to belong to the Rāshṭrakūṭa dynasty. Such connections are even now allowed. Care is only taken that the bride should not be the grand-daughter (daughter's daughter) of the same sub-clan to which the bridgroom belongs.

(5) First of all, the objection has no sound basis. Secondly, the inscription, dated 1166 (A.D. 1109), of the prince regent Gōvindachandra contains:—

प्रध्वस्ते सूर्यसोमोद्भवविदितमहाक्षत्रवंशद्वयेऽस्मिन्
उत्सन्नप्रायवेदध्वनिजगदखिलं मन्यमानः स्वयंभूः ॥
कृत्वा देहग्रहाय प्रवणमिह मनः शुद्धबुद्धिर्धरित्र्यां
उद्धर्तुं धर्ममार्गान् प्रथितमिह तथा क्षत्रवंशद्वयं च ॥
वंशे तत्र ततः सएष समभूद् भूपालचूडामणिः
प्रध्वस्तोद्धतवैरिवीरतिमिरः श्रीचन्द्रदेवो नृपः ॥

i.e, on the expiry of the kings of the Sōlar and the Lunar dynasties, when the Vēdic religion began to dwindle away, Bramhā himself, with a view to maintain all these, took an incarnation in the person of king Chandradēva in this family.

---

1 The ruler of Kotāh, belonging to the Chauhāna dynasty, is known to the general public as of the Hādā clan, which is a branch of the Chauhāna dynasty.

2 Epigraphia Indica, Vol. IX, pages 319-328.

This shows that, at that time also, the Gāhaḍavāla family was held in very high esteem.

By taking all these facts into consideration we conclude that "Gahaḍavāla" was a branch[1] of the Rashṭrakūṭa dynasty. This subject has already been dealt with in the chapter "The Rashṭrakūṭas and the Gāhaḍavālas."

---

1 Some people are of opinion that just as the Chūṇḍāvata, Ūdāvata and Jagamālōta branches are found in both the Rāṭhōras and the Sisōdiyās, in the same manner, it is possible that a distinct branch named "Yādava" might have ensued from the Rāṭhōra dynasty, and afterwards people might have connected it with king Sātyaki due to a particular member of the branch having the same name. But just as the names of certain branches of the Rāṭhōras and Sīsōdiyās, being the same, the two dynasties are yet quite distinct; even so the famous Yādavas of the Lunar dynasty and the supposed Yādava branch of Rāṭhōras are distinct from each other. This subject has already been discussed under the chapter "The Origin of the Rāshṭrakūṭas." Moreover, even in the modern times there are many branches such as Nāgadā, Dāhimā, Sōnagarā, Shrīmālī, Gauḍa, etc., which are common to the Brahamṇas, Kshatriyas and Vaishyas.

THE RELIGION
OF
THE RĀSHṬRAKŪṬAS.

In the earliest copper grant of the Rashṭrakūṭa king Abhimanyu an image of a lion, the vehicle of 'Ambikā,' is impressed. In the seal of the copper grant of Dantivarman (Dantidurga II), of Shaka S. 675 (V.S. 810=A.D. 753), there is the impression of an image of 'Shiva.' In the coins of Krishṇarāja I his title is mentioned as 'Parama Māhēshvara' and in his inscription of Shaka S. 690 (V. S. 825=A. D. 768) there is an impression* of a 'Shiva Linga.' But of the copper grants of the later dates some bear the impression of an image of a "Garuḍa", while others that of 'Shiva.'

The flag of the Rāshṭrakūṭas was called the "Pālidhvaja"[1] and they were also known as "Ōka Kētu". Their coat of arms contained the signs of the Ganges and the Jamuna, probably copied from the western Chālukyas of Bādāmī.

---

1 In the 22nd 'Parva' of the 'Ādi Purāṇa,' written by Jinasēna, it is said:—

स्रग्वस्त्रबर्हिसाब्जहंसवीनमृगाशिनाम् ।
वृषभेभेन्द्रचक्राणां ध्वजाः स्युर्दशभेदकाः ॥२१९॥
अष्टोत्तरशतं ज्ञेयाः प्रत्येकं पालिकेतनाः ।
एकैकस्यां दिशि प्रोच्चैस्तरंगास्तोयधेरिव ॥२२०॥

i.e., flags are of 10 kinds according to the signs, *viz.*, 1. Garland, 2. Cloth, 3. Peacock, 4. Lotus, 5. Swan, 6 Garuḍa, 7. Lion, 8. Bull, 9. Elephant and 10. Quoit. And a 'Pālikētana' or 'Pālidhvaja' is a flag which contains in the 4 directions 108 flags of each of these 10 kinds, or 1080 × 4=4320 flags in all the four directions.

The family deity of the later Rāshṭrakūṭas is known by the names of "Lātanā" (Lāṭāṇā), "Rāshṭrashyēnā,"[1] "Manasā" or "Vindhyavāsinī." It is said that as this goddess, having incarnated as a falcon, had saved their kingdom, she became known by the name of 'Rāshṭrashyēnā.' In commemoration of the above event a falcon is represented on the "State Flag" of the Marwar Darbar even upto the present day.

From the above it appears that the kings of this dynasty from time to time used to observe the 'Shaiva,' the 'Vaishṇava,' and the 'Shākta' religions.

The 'Uttara Purāṇa' of the Jainas contains the following:—

यस्य प्रांशु नखांशुजालविसरद्धारान्तराविर्भव-
त्पादांभोजरजःपिशङ्गमुकुटप्रत्यग्ररत्नद्युतिः ।
संस्मर्ता स्वममोघवर्षनृपतिः पूतोऽहमद्येत्यलं
स श्रीमाञ्जिनसेनपूज्यभगवत्पादो जगन्मङ्गलम् ॥

i.e., king Amōghavarsha, having bowed before the Jaina priest Jinasēna, congratulated himself. This shows that Amōghavarsha was the follower of the teachings of Jinasēna. In the book named "Ratnamālikā" ("Prashṇōttararatnamalikā"), written by Amōghavarsha, it is said:—

प्रणिपत्य वर्धमानं प्रश्नोत्तररत्नमालिकां वक्ष्ये ।
नागनरामरवन्द्यं देवं देवाधिपं वीरम् ॥
....

1 In the 11th chapter of the 'Ēkalinga Māhātmya' it is stated:—

स्वदेहाद्राष्ट्रश्येनां तां सृष्ट्वा स्थाप्याऽथ तत्र सा ॥१५॥
....
श्येनारूपं समास्थाय देवो राष्ट्रं त्राहि त्रायतो वज्रहस्ता ॥१६॥
....
दुष्टग्रहेभ्योन्यतमेभ्य एव श्येने त्राणं मेदपाटस्य कार्यम् ॥१७॥
....

राष्ट्रश्येनेति नाम्नीयं मेदपाटस्य रक्षणम् ।
करोति न च भङ्गोऽस्य यवनेभ्यो मनागपि ॥२२॥

This shows that the protectress of Mewar is also the very Goddess Rāshṭrashyēnā.' Its temple is situated on the top of a hill at a distance of 3 miles from the temple of 'Ēkalinga Mahādēva' in Mewar.

विवेकात्त्यक्तराज्येन राज्ञेयं रत्नमालिका ।
रचिताऽमोघवर्षेण सुधियां सदलङ्कृतिः ॥

i.e., having bowed to Varddhamana (Mahāvīra) I write this 'Prashnōttarararatnamalikā.'

Amōghavarsha, who renounced the kingdom because of 'Jnāna' (discrimination), has written this book named "Ratnamālikā."

In the "Gaṇitasarasangraha" of Mahāvīrāchārya it is stated:—

प्रीणितः प्राणिशस्यौघो निरीतिर्निरवग्रहः ।
श्रीमताऽमोघवर्षेण येन स्वेष्टहितैषिणा ॥१॥

....

विध्वस्तैकान्तपक्षस्य स्याद्वादन्यायवादिनः ।
देवस्य नृपतुङ्गस्य वर्धतां तस्य शासनम् ॥६॥

i.e., the subjects under the rule of Amōghavarsha are happy and the land yields plenty of grain. May the kingdom of this king (Nripatunga-Amōghavarsha), the follower of Jainism, ever increase far and wide.

This also shows that Amōghavarsha was the follower of Jainism and presumably he embraced this religion in his old age.

It is quite clear that the 'Paurāṇik' religion had flourished to a great extent during the reign of the Rāshṭrakūṭa kings, and many temples, dedicated to 'Shiva' and 'Vishṇu', were built. All the rock-cut temples, etc., built before the reign of the Rāshṭrakūṭas of the Deccan, were meant for the Budhists, Jainas and the Nirgranthas only. But it was in the time of these kings that the 'Kailāsa Bhavana' of the Ellōrā caves, dedicated to 'Shiva,' was constructed for the first time.

Most of the kings of the Kanauj branch of this family were the followers of Vaishnavism and their copper grants found upto this date show that this dynasty was more generous than all the other ruling dynasties.

SCIENCE AND ARTS
IN THE TIME OF
THE RĀSHṬRAKŪṬAS.

Much improvement was effected in science and arts in the time of the Rāshṭrakūṭa kings.

These kings were themselves men of learning and always patronised it. The logician Akalanka Bhaṭṭa, author of the "Rājavārtika", the "Nyāyavinishchaya," the "Ashṭashatī" and the "Laghīyastraya"; Mahāvīrachārya, author of the "Gaṇitasārasangraha"; Jinasēna, writer of the "Ādī Purāṇa" and the "Pārshvābhyudaya"; another Jinasēna, author of the "Harivamsha Puraṇa"; Guṇabhadrāchārya, writer of the "Ātmānushāsana"; poet Halāyudha, compiler of the "Kavirahasya[1]"; Sōmadēva Sūri, writer of the "Yashastilaka Champu" and the "Nītivākyāmrita" on politics; Canarese poet Pōnna, writer of the "Shānti Purāṇa" (whom king Krishṇa III, had honoured with the title of "Ubhayabhāshā Chakravartī" = master of two languages; Pushpadanta, writer of the "Yashōdhara Charita", the "Nāgakumāra Charita" and the "Jaina Mahā Purāṇa"; Trivikrama Bhaṭṭa, author of the "Madālasā Champū"; Lākshmīdhara, compiler of the "Vyavahāra Kalpataru"; and Shrī Harsha, author of the "Naishadhīya Charita" and the "Khaṇḍana khaṇḍa khādya"and others, flourished in the time of these kings.[2]

1 Sir Bhaṇḍārkar inclines to identify the author of the "Kavirahasya" with the Halāyudha, who wrote the 'Abhidhāna ratnamālā,' but Weber places the latter about the end of the 11th century.

2 In the Jaina library of Karanjā there is a book named "Jvālā malinī kalpa." This book was completed in Shaka S. 861 during the reign of Krishna III.

The "Prashṇōttararatnamālikā", written by king Amōghavarsh, which exists even to this day, testifies to the learning of the kings of this dynasty. Its composition is of a very high order. Though some persons think Shankarāchārya, and others 'Shvētāmbara' Jainācharya, to be the author of the book, yet in the copies of the book, written by 'Digambara Jainas,' it is said to have been compiled by king Amōghavarsha and the same fact is proved by the verses quoted from the book in the preceding chapter. This book has also been translated into the Tibetan language, in which, too, the name of the author is written as Amōghavarsha.

The same Amōghavarsha had also written another book named "Kavirājamārga", a prosody, in the Canarese language.

We have already stated that art also had much improved in their times. The temple of 'Kailāsa Bhavana'[1] of the Ellōrā caves is a living instance of the fact. This cave temple was constructed in the reign of king Krishṇarāja I by cutting the rocks. Its excellence is beyond the power of description.

"Jayaḍhavalā", a commentary of the principles of the 'Digambara' branch of Jainism, was written in the time of Amōghavarsha I. From the "Shrikanṭha charita" of poet Mankha, it appears that Alankāra, the minister of king Jayasimha of Kāshmīr, had called a big assembly in which Pandit Suhala was sent out as a delegate by king Gōvindachandra of Kanauj.

अन्यः स सुहलस्तेन ततोऽवन्यत पण्डितः ।
दूतो गोविन्दचन्द्रस्य कान्यकुब्जस्यभूभुजः ।
(सर्ग २५ श्लो० १०२)

1 Of the Ajantā caves, which are famous for their art, Nos. 1 and 2 were also built in the beginning of the reign of the Rāshṭrakūṭas of Mānyakhēṭa.

THE GLORY
OF
THE EARLY RĀSHṬRAKŪṬAS.

In the "Silsilātuttavārīkh"[1], a history written by an Arab trader Sulaimān, in A. H. 237 (V. S. 908=A.D. 851) and modified and completed by Abūzaīdul Hasan of Sirāf, in A. H. 303 (V. S. 973=A.D. 916), it is thus stated:—

"The inhabitants of India and China agree that there are four great or principal kings in the world. They place the king of the Arabs (Khalif of Baghdād) at the head of these........The king of China reckons himself next after the king of the Arabs. After him comes the king of the Greeks, and lastly the Balharā, prince of the men who have their ears pierced (*i.e.*, the Hindus)".

"The Balharā is the most eminent of the princes of India, and the Indians acknowledge his superiority. Every prince in India is master in his own state, but all pay homage to the supermacy of Balharā. The representatives sent by the Balharā to other princes are received with most profound respect in order to show him honour. He gives regular pay to his troops, as the practice is among the Arabs. He has many horses and elephants, and immense wealth. The coins which pass in his country are the Tātārīya dirhams, each of which weighs a dirham and a half of the coinage of the king. They are dated from the year in which the

1 Elliot's History of India, Vol. I, pages 3-4.

dynasty acquired the throne. They do not, like the Arabs, use the Hijra of the prophet, but date their eras from the beginning of their kings' reigns; and their kings live long, frequently reigning for fifty years. The inhabitants of the Balharā's country say that if their kings reign and live for a long time, it is solely in consequence of the favour shown to the Arabs. In fact, among all the kings there is no one to be found who is so partial to the Arabs as the Balharā; and his subjects follow his example."

"Balharā is the title borne by all the kings of this dynasty. It is similar to Chosroes (of the Persians), and is not a proper name. The kingdom of the Balharā commences on the seaside, at the country of kukam (Konkan) on the tongue of land which stretches to China. The Balharā has around him several kings with whom he is at war, but whom he greatly excels. Among them is the king of the Jurz[1].

In the book "Kitāb-ul-Masālik-ul-Mumālik", written by Ibn Khurdādbā, who died in A. H. 300 (V. S. 969= A. D. 912), it is thus stated:[2]—

"The greatest king of India is Balhārā, whose name imports "king of kings." He wears a ring in which

1 The above statement seems to be a sketch of the reign of king Amōghavarsha I who was ruling in the Deccan when this book was written and who had also attacked Rāshṭrakūṭa king Dhruvarāja I of Gujrat. The kingdom of the Rāshṭrakūṭa king Dhruvarāja I of the Deccan extended from Rāmēshvara in the south to Ayōdhyā in the north. In the Chronology of Nēpāl it is stated that in Shaka S. 811 (V. S. 946=A.D. 889) Kyānadēva, the founder of the dynasty of Karṇāṭik, having come up from the Deccan, took the whole of Nēpāl and for 6 generations his descendants ruled there. In Shaka Samvat 811 Krishṇarāja II was the king of Karṇāṭik; and seventh in descent from him was Karkarāja II from whom Tailapa II of the Chālukya dynasty seized the kingdom of the Rāshṭrakūṭas. So, it is probable that the descendants of Dhruvarāja I of Mānyakhēṭa, having progressed beyond Ayōdhyā, might have captured a portion of Nēpāl and afterwards Krishṇarāja II, having advanced farther, taken the whole of the country. As the boundaries of China and Nēpāl are adjacent, Sulaimān might have, for this reason, recorded the extent of their kingdom to be upto the Chinese frontier.

2 Elliots History of India, Vol. I, page 13. This description refers to the reign of king Krishṇarāja II.

is inscribed the following sentence:—"What is begun with resolution ends with success."

The book named "Murūjul Zahab", written by Al-Masūdi about A. H. 332 (V. S. 1001=A.D. 944), contains the following:[1]—

"The city of Mānkīr, which was the great centre of India, submitted to a king called the Balharā, and the name of this prince continues to his successors who reign in that capital until the present time (332 A.H.)."

"The greatest of the kings of India in our time is the Balharā, sovereign of the city of Mānkīr. Many of the kings of India turn their faces towards him in their prayers, and they make supplications to his ambassadors, who come to visit them. The kingdom of the Balharā is bordered by many other countries of India. ..The capital of the Balharā is eighty Sindi Parasangs from the sea, (and the Parasang[2] is equal to eight miles). His troops and elephants are innumerable, but his troops are mostly infantry, because the seat of his government is among the mountains...Bayūra[3] who is the king of Kanauj, is an enemy of the Balharā, the king of India....The inhabitants of Mānkīr, which is the capital of the Balharā, speak the Kirīya[4] language, which has this name from Kira the place where it is spoken."

Al Istakhrī,[5] who wrote the "Kitābul Akālīm", in A. H. 340 (V. S. 1008=A.D. 951) as also Ibn Haukal,[6] who came to India between A. H. 331 and 358 (A.D. 943 and 968) and wrote the "Ashkal-ul-Bilād" in A. H. 366 (A.D.=976), say:—

---

1 Elliot's History of India, Vol. I, pages 19-24. This refers to Krishṇarāja III.

2 A "Farasang" is equal to three miles but Sir Elliot has taken it to be equal to 8 miles.

3 This seems to be a corrupt form of Pratihāra.

4 Perhaps the same is now called the Canarese language.

5 Elliot's History of India, Vol. I, page 27.

6 Elliot's History of India, Vol. I, page 34.

"From Kambaya[1] to Saimur[2] is the land of the Balharā, and in it there are several Indian kings. The city in which the Balharā resides is Mānkīr, which has an extensive territory."

From the above extracts, taken from the writings of the Arabian travellers, we conclude that at that time the power of the Rāshṭrakūṭa kings had reached its zenith.

The Rāhshṭrakūṭa king Dantidurga defeated Sōlankī (Chālukya) 'Vallabha' Kīrtivarman and assumed the title of 'Vallabharāja,' which was also attached to the names of all his successors.[3] It is therefore that the aforesaid Arabian writers have mentioned these kings as Balharā, a corrupt form of "Vallabharāja."[4]

From the inscription of the Sōmēshvara temple, near Yēvūr (Deccan), it appears that there were 800 elephants in the army of Rāshṭrakūṭa king Indra, and that 500 feudatory chiefs followed as his retinue.[5]

---

1 Cambay.

2 Presumably this city was on the border of Sind to which we can trace the northern boundary of the kingdom of the Rāshṭrakūṭas.

3 Sir Henry Elliot, Col. Tod and others suppose that the Arab writers had used the word Balharā for the kings of Balabhī or for the Chālukya kings themselves, (Elliot's History of India, Vol. I, pages 354-355). But these suppositions are groundless as the Balabhī kingdom had come to an end about V. S. 823 (A.D. 766); and the Chālukya kingdom had been split up into two branches on the death of the Chālukya king Mangalīsha in V. S. 667 (A.D. 610). Pulakēshin was the head of one of them and Rāshṭrakūṭa Dantidurga seized his kingdom from his descendant Kīrtivarman between V.S. 805 and 810 (A.D 748 and 753). It remained under the Rāshṭrakūṭa dynasty upto V. S. 1030 (A D. 973) about which time it was regained by Chālukya Tailapa II from Rāshṭrakūṭa king Karkarāja II. Thus, about V. S. 805 to 1030 (A.D 748 to 973) the kingdom of the western branch of the Chālukyas remained in the possession of the Rāshṭrakūṭas. Formerly, the capital of this branch of the Sōlankīs was Bādāmi. But later, Tailapa II shifted it to Kalyāṇī. The second branch was headed by Vishṇuvardhana, whose descendants were called Eastern Chālukyas. They ruled at Vēngī and were the feudatories of the Rāshṭrakūṭas.

4 Just as in the Persian histories the title Rāṇā of the kings of Mewar is used instead of their names; similarly, the Arab writers have used the hereditary title Balharā (Vallabharāja) of the Rāshṭrakūṭa kings of the Deccan instead of their names.

5 यो राष्ट्रकूटकुलमिन्द्रइतिप्रसिद्धं कृष्णाह्वयस्य सुतमष्टशतेभसैन्यम्
निर्जित्य दग्धनृपपंचशतो........................

'Indian Antiquary, Vol. VIII, pages 12.

In the copper grant,[1] dated Shaka S. 852 (V. S. 987= A.D. 930), of Gōvinda IV, it is stated that the Rāshṭrakūṭa king Indrarāja III crossed the Ganges with his cavalry and laid waste the city of Kanauj.

A copper grant,[2] dated Shaka S. 915 (V.S. 1050=A.D. 993), of the ruler of the Shilāhāra dynasty of Thānā, contains:—

चोलो लोलोऽभियाभूद्गजपतिरपतन्मानतो गह्वरान्तः,
वाङ्गीशश्चासशेषः समभवदभवच्छैलरन्ध्रे तथान्ध्रः ।
पाण्ड्येशः स्त्रगिडतोऽभूदनुजलधिजलं द्वीपपालाः प्रलीनाः,
यस्मिन् दत्तप्रयाणे सकलमपि तदा राजकं न व्यराजत् ॥

i.e., when king Krishṇarāja III mobilized his armies, the kings of the Chōla, Bengāl, Kanauj, Āndhra and Pāṇḍya countries used to quiver.

In the same grant the extent of the sovereignty of king Krishṇarāja III is stated to be from Himālayas in the north to Ceylon in the south, and from eastern sea in the east to the western sea in the west.

About V. S. 1030=(A.D. 973) the Chālukya king Tailapa II defeated the Rāshṭrakūṭa king Karkarāja and overthrew the Rāshṭrakūṭa kingdom of Mānyakhēṭa. The copper grant referred to above was issued after this event. This shows that the power of the Rāshṭrakūṭa kings was once very great, so much so, that their feudatories indulged in referring to their glories even after their fall.

The country under the sway of the Rāshṭrakūṭas was called "Raṭṭa Pāṭī" or "Raṭṭa Rājya" and consist-

---

1 यस्माद्यद्द्विपदन्तघातविषमं कालप्रियप्राङ्गणं
तीर्णा यत्तुरगैरगाधयमुना सिन्धुप्रतिस्पर्धिनी ॥
येनेदं हि महोदयारिनगरं निर्मूलमुन्मूलितं
नाम्नाद्यापि जनैः कुशस्थलमिति ख्यातिं परां नीयते ॥

Epigraphia Indica, Vol. VII, page 36.

2 History of Mediaeval Hindu India, Vol. II, page 349.

ed of 7 lacs of villages and towns as is mentioned in the 'Skanda Purāṇa'[1]:—

ग्रामाणां सप्तलक्षं च रट्टराज्ये प्रकीर्तितम् ।

i.e., the kingdom of the Raṭṭas (Rāshṭrakūṭas) consisted of 7 lacs of villages.

The military band called "Tivalī" was a speciality of their processions.

We learn from the copper grant,[2] dated V. S. 1161 (A.D. 1104), of Gōvindachandra, found at Basāhī, that it was Chandradēva of the Gāhaḍavāla branch of the Rāshṭrakūṭa family, who had restored order by suppressing the anarchy that had resulted on the deaths of kings Karṇa and Bhōja. It also refers that Gōvindachandra had granted in charity the village of Basahi (Basāhī) together with the 'Turushkaḍaṇḍa,'[3] (cess levied upon the Mohmmedans), which shows that just as the Mohammedan kings levied 'Jaziyā' upon the non-Mohammedans, in the like manner, Madnapāla levied a tax upon the Muslims. This proves his power and glory. As regards Jayachchandra it is stated in the 'Rambhāmanjarī Nāṭikā' that he defeated the Chandēla king Madnavarmadēva of Kālinjar, possessed an exceptionally large army and ruled over the territory between the Ganges and the Jamuna.

---

1 "Skanda Purāṇa,' Kaumārikā Khaṇḍa, Adhyaya 39, verse 135.

2 याते श्रीभोजभूपे विबुधवरवधूनेत्रसीमातिथित्वं
श्रीकर्णे कीर्तिशेषं गतवति च नृपे क्ष्मात्यये जायमाने ।
भर्तारं याव [ध] रित्री त्रिदिवविभुनिभं प्रीतियोगादुपेता
त्राता विश्वासपूर्वं समभवदिह स क्ष्मापतिश्चन्द्रदेवः ॥

King Karṇa referred to here was Karṇa of the 'Haihaya' (Kalachuri) clan, who was alive in V. S. 1099. But there is a controversy about king Bhōja referred to here. Some say that it was the Paramāra king Bhōja who died about V. S. 1110 and others think it to be the Pratihāra Bhōja II, who lived about V. S. 980.

3 In the copper grant, dated V. S. 1186 (A.D. 1129), of Gōvindachandra, found in Oudh, there is also a mention of this 'Turushkaḍaṇḍa.'

Lucknow Museum Report of (1914-15), pages 4 and 10.

CONCLUSION.

Taking all the foregoing facts into consideration we conclude that in the earlier period a branch of the Rāshṭrakūṭas came down to Kanauj, where they established a kingdom, which in the course of time became weak. After this the Guptas, the Baisas, the Maukharīs and the Pratihāras in succession ruled over it. About Vikrama Samvat 1137 (A. D. 1080) another branch of Rāashṭrakūṭas, once again, conquered Kanauj and established their kingdom.

This branch, being connected with the 'Gādhipura,' (Kanauj) afterwards came to be known by the name of "Gāhaḍavāla." In V.S. 1250 (A.D. 1194) Jayachchandra, the Gāhaḍavāla king of Kanauj, was attacked by Shahābuddīn Ghōrī and lost his life. When Shahābuddīn went back after plundering the town, Harishchandra, the son of Jayachchandra, succeeded his father. Though not powerful he was able to retain Kanauj and its neighbouring districts in his possession for some years. But when Qutubuddīn Aibak and after him Shamsuddīn Altamash took the country and put an end to the independent kingdom of the Rāshṭrakūṭas, of this branch, Rāo Sīhā, the grandson of Jayachchandra, left Kanauj and remained for sometime in Mahuī.[1] Later, when this district was also taken by the Mohammedans, Sīhā (after roaming about for a time) came to Marwar about V. S. 1268.

The descendants of Rāo Sīhā are at present ruling over the States of Mārwār, Bīkānēr, Īdar, Kishangarh, Ratlām, Sītāmaū, Sailānā and Jhābuā.

---

1 It is stated in the 'Āīn-i-akabarī' that Sīhā lived at Khōr (Shamsābād) and was killed there.

According to our opinion the genealogical table from Vijayachandra to Sīhā is as follows:—

Vijayachandra.
- Jayachchandra.
  - Harishchandra (Bardāīsēna)[1] (Prahasta).
    - Sētarāma.
    - Sīhā.
  - Jayapāla (Jajapāla).
- Māṇikachandra.

The third branch of the Rāshṭrakūṭas, which had gone down to the Deccan, turned out the Sōlankīs and founded a kingdom there. Though we have not yet been able to trace the date of the commencement of this kingdom, yet it is clear that in the time of Chālukya Jayasimha, (in the later half of the sixth century of the Vikrama era) there existed in the Deccan a powerful kingdom of the Rāshṭrakūṭas. It was overthrown by the said Jayasimha when he set up the Sōlankī kingdom there. But about 250 years after this, *i.e.*, about V.S. 805=A.D. 747), Dantivarman II defeated Sōlankī Kīrtivarman II and re-established the Rāshṭrakūṭa kingdom in the Deccan. This kingdom lasted for about 225 years, upto V.S. 1030 (A.D. 973), when Sōlankī Tailapa II again overthrew it and defeated Karkarāja II, its last king.

Two branches of the Deccan family of the Rāshṭrakūṭas had ruled over "Lāṭa" (Gujrat) from the beginning of the 8th century of the Vikrama era upto the first half of the 9th century. They were the feudatories of the Rāshṭrakūṭa kings of the Deccan.

Proofs about the rule of the branches of the old Rāshṭrakūṭas in Saundattī (Dharwar—Bombay), Hathūndī (Marwar) and Dhanōp (Shahpurā) have also been found.

Mention of some more inscriptions, etc., of the Rāshṭrakūṭas, found here and there, will be made in the next chapter.

1 Possibly Baradāisēna may be a younger brother of Harishchandra.

MISCELLANEOUS INSCRIPTIONS

OF THE

RĀSHṬRAKŪṬAS.

The earliest known record of the Rāshṭrakūṭas is the copper grant of king Abhimanyu.[1] From its characters it appears to be of about the beginning of the 7th century of the Vikrama era. In the seal of it the image of a lion, the vehicle of Goddess Durgā, is impressed.

It refers to a charitable grant made at Mānpur for the worship of God 'Shiva' and contains the following genealogical table of the kings:—

Mānānka.
|
Dēvarāja.
|
Bhavishya.
|
Abhimanyu.

The seat of Government of Abhimanyu was Mānpur, which is considered by some scholars to be the modern Mānpur (12 miles south-west of Mhow in Malwa).

Two more grants of the Rāshtrakūtas have been found at the village of Multai (Bētūl district, C.P.); the first[2] of which is of Shaka S. 553 (V.S. 688=A.D. 631) and contains the following genealogy:—

Durgarāja.
|
Gōvindarāja.
|
Svāmikarāja.
|
Nannarāja.

---

1 Epigraphia Indica, Vol. VIII, page 164.
2 Do. do. XI. page 276.

The other[1] is of Shaka Samvat 631 (V.S. 766=A.D. 709) of the time of Rāshṭrakūṭa king Nandarāja and contains the following genealogy:—

Durgarāja.[2]
|
Gōvindarāja.
|
Svāmikarāja.
|
Nandarāja.

In this grant the title of Nandarāja is mentioned as "Yuddha Shūra" and the charity mentioned in it was granted on the 15th day of the bright half of Kārtika. If the Shaka Samvat mentioned in it be considered as the past one, then the date of the grant falls on the 24th October A.D. 709.

In both the aforesaid copper grants the first three names of the genealogical tables are similar, but there is some slight difference in the fourth name. Taking into consideration the dates of the two inscriptions we think that Nandarāja of the second inscription might be a younger brother of Nannarāja of the first and succeeded him on his death.

In the seals of these grants there are the images of "Garuḍa."

An inscription of V. S. 917[3] (A.D. 860) has been found at village of Pathārī in the Bhōpāl State, which contains the genealogical table of the Rāshṭrakūṭa kings of Central India as follows:—

Jējjaṭa.
|
Karkarāja.
|
Parabala (V. S. 917).

---

1 Indian Antiquary, Vol. XVIII, page 234.

2 It is probable that this Durgarāja is a second name of king Dantivarman I of the Deccan, because, firstly, the period of Durgarāja of this inscription synchronises with that of Dantivarman I. Secondly, Dantivarman's second name was Dantidurga which almost resembles Durgarāja and thirdly, in the inscription of the Dashāvatāra temple the name of Dantivarman II is written as Dantidurgarāja. If this supposition be correct then the Gōvindarāja of this inscription would be a younger brother of Rāshṭrakūṭa Indrarāja I of the Deccan.

3 Epigraphia Indica, Vol. IX, page 248.

Raṇṇādēvī, the daughter of king Parabala, was married[1] to king Dharmapāla of the Pāla dynasty of 'Gauḍa' (Bengal). Karkarāja, the father of Parabala defeated Nāgabhaṭa (Nāgāvalōka) who was probably the son of the Pratihāra king Vatsarāja. An inscription[2] of Nāgabhaṭa, dated V. S. 872 (A.D. 815), has been found at the village of Buchkalā (Bīlārā district) in Mārwār. But Professor Kielhorn identifies him with the Nāgāvalōka[3] of the Bhrigukachchha grant of V. S. 813 (A.D. 756).

An inscription[4] of the Rāshṭrakūṭas found at Bōdha Gayā contains the following genealogy:—

Nanna (Guṇāvalōka).
|
Kīrtirāja.
|
Tunga (Dharmāvalōka).

Bhāgyadēvī, the daughter of Tunga, was married to Rājyapāla[5] of the Pāla dynasty, who was fourth in descent from the aforesaid Dharmapāla. The inscription bears the year 15, which might be the 15th regnal year of king Tunga who probably lived about V. S. 1025 (A.D. 968).

---

1 Bhārata-kē-Prāchīna Rājavamsha, Vol. I, page 185.
2 Epigraphia Indica, Vol. IX, page 198.
3 This Nāgāvalōka was probably Pratihāra Nāgabhaṭa I.
4 Bōdha Gayā, (by Rājēndralāl Mittra), page 195.
5 Bhārata-kē-Prāchīna Rājavamsha, Vol. I, page 189.

An inscription of the time of Lakhanapāla[1] has been discovered from Badāūn, which is probably of about V. S. 1258 (A.D. 1201). It contains the following genealogical table:—

- Chandra.
  - Vigrahapāla.
    - Bhuvanapālā.
      - Gōpāla.
        - Tribhuvanapāla.
        - Madanapāla.
        - Dēvapāla.
          - Bhīmapāla.
            - Shūrapāla.
              - Amritapāla.
              - Lakhanapāla.

This inscription indicates that Chandra was the first Rāshṭrakūṭa king who took the town of Badāūn, which is stated to be the ornament of the kingdom of Kanauj.

THE RĀSHṬRAKŪṬAS OF MĀNYAKHĒṬA (Deccan)

FROM BEFORE V. S. 650 (A.D. 593) TO ABOUT V. S. 1039 (A.D. 982).

In an inscription found at Yēvūr and also in a copper grant[1] of the Sōlankīs found at Miraj, it is thus stated:—

यो राष्ट्रकूटकुलमिन्द्र इति प्रसिद्धं
कृष्णाह्वयस्य सुतमष्टशतेभसैन्यम् ।
निर्जित्य दग्धनृपपंचशतो बभार
भूयश्चुलुक्यकुलवल्लभराजलक्ष्मीम् ॥
....
तद्भवो विक्रमादित्यः कीर्तिवर्मा तदात्मजः
येन चालुक्यराज्यश्रीरन्तरायिण्यभूद्भुवि ।

i.e., he (Sōlankī Jayasimha) by defeating Rāshṭrakūṭa Indra, the owner of 800 elephants and son of Krishṇa, re-established the kingdom of Vallabharāja (Sōlankīs). (From the word Vallabharāja mentioned in this inscription it appears that this title originally belonged to the Sōlankīs and after defeating them the Rāshṭrakūṭas assumed it. Therefore, the Arab writers have mentioned the Rashṭrakūṭa kings as "Balharās" which is a corrupt form of the word "Vallabharāja").

In the time of Kīrtivarman II, son of Vikramāditya, (who was 11th in descent from this Jayasimha) the Sōlankī kingdom was again overthrown.

From the aforesaid stanzas it appears that the Rāshṭrakūṭas ruled in the Deccan before it was conquered by Sōlankī Jayasimha in the latter part of the sixth century of the Vikrama era. But between V. S.

1 Indian Antiquary, Vol. VIII, pages 12-14.

805 and 810 (A.D. 747 and 753) the Rāshṭrakūṭa king Dantidurga II again seized a large part of the kingdom from Sōlankī Kīrtivarman II.

The history of the Rāshṭrakūṭa family, to which this Dantidurga II belonged, is traced through inscriptions, copper grants and Sanskrit books as follows:—

1. DANTIVARMAN (DANTIDURGA I).

This king was a descendant of Indra, son of Krishṇa, mentioned above. He is the first king known through the inscriptions of the Rāshṭkūṭas of this line. In the inscription[1] of the Dashāvatāra temple, he is described as a protector of 'Varṇāshrama Dharma' (laws of castes and stages of life). He was a good-natured, merciful and independent ruler. He probably flourished before V.S. 650 (A.D. 593).

2. INDRARĀJA I.

He was the son and successor of Dantivarman. His and his father's names have been taken from the inscription of the Dashāvatāra temple in the Ellōrā caves, in which after Dantidurga II, the name of Mahārāja Sharva[2] is mentioned. But in other inscriptions of this branch of the Rāshṭrakūṭas, the names of Dantivarman I and Indrarāja I, are not found, for the pedigrees in them commence from Gōvinda I.

In the aforesaid Dashāvatāra inscription, this Indra is described as a performer of many sacrifices (Yagyas) and a brave king. Prachchhakarāja appears to be his second name.

1 Archaeological Survey report of Western India, Vol. V, page 87; and cave temples inscriptions, page 92.

2 It is not clear who is meant by "Sharva" here. Some think "Sharva" to be a brother of Dantidurga and others take it for Amōghavarsha. From the aforesaid Dashāvatāra inscription it appears that this "Sharva" camped in this temple with his army. Probably "Sharva" was a title or another name of Dantidurga.

3. GŌVINDARĀJA I.

He was the son of Indrarāja and ascended the throne after his death. We learn from the inscription[1] of Pulakēshin II, dated Shaka S. 556 (V.S. 691=A.D. 634) found at Ēhōlē, that at the time when Mangalīsha was killed, and his nephew Pulakēshīn II succeeded him, Gōvindarāja with the aid of his allies, taking opportunity of the consequent weakness of the Sōlankīs, attempted to regain the lost kingdom of his ancestors. But as he could not succeed, he concluded peace.[2]

It appears, therefore, that Gōvindarāja was a contemporary of Pulakēshīn II and should have lived about V. S. 691 (A.D. 634).

"Vīra Nārāyaṇa" was another name of Gōvindarāja.

4. KARKARĀJA (KAKKA I).

He was the son and successor of Gōvindarāja I. The Brahmaṇas had performed several sacrifices during his reign, as this generous king himself was a follower of the Vedic religion and a patron of learning. He had three sons:—Indrarāja, Krishṇarāja and Nanna.

5. INDRARĀJA II.

He was the eldest son and successor of Karkarāja. His queen was a daughter of the Sōlankī (Chālukya) dynasty and her mother was born of the Lunar race. This shows that, at that time, the Rāshṭrakūṭas and the western Chālukyas were not, in any way, on unfriendly terms.

---

1 Epigraphia Indica, Vol. VI, pages 5-6.

2 लब्ध्वा कालं भुवमुपगते जेतुमप्यायिकाख्ये
गोविन्दे च द्विरदनिकरैरुत्तराम्भ्योधिरथ्या ।
यस्यानीकैर्युधि भयरसज्ञत्वमेकः प्रयातः
तत्रावाप्तं फलमुपकृतस्यापरेणापि सद्यः ॥

His army consisted of a considerable number of horses and elephants.

6. DANTIVARMAN. (DANTIDURGA II).

He was the son and successor of Indrarāja II. Between V.S. 804 and 810 (A.D. 748 and 753) he took possession of Vātāpī, the northern portion of the kingdom of Chālukya (Sōlankī) Kīrtivarman II, and again established the Rāshṭrakūṭa kingdom in the Deccan, which remained under this dynasty for about 225 years.

A copper grant[1] of Shaka S. 675 (V. S. 810=A.D. 753), found at Sāmangaḍh (Kolhāpur State), contains the following lines:—

माही महानदी रेवा रोधोभित्तिविदारणं
....
यो वल्लभं सपदि दंडलके (बले) न जित्वा
राजाधिराजपरमेश्वरतामुपैति ।
कांचीशकेरलनराधिपचोलपाण्ड्य—
श्रीहर्षवज्रटविभेदविधानदक्षम् ।
कर्णाटकं बलमनन्तमजेयरत्यै (ष्यै) [2]
भ्रि (भृ) त्यैः कियद्भिरपि यः सहसा जिगाय ॥

i.e., his (Dantivarman II's) elephants had gone up to the Māhī, the Mahānadī and the Narmadā.[3]

Defeating Vallabha (western Chālukya king Kīrtivarman II) he assumed the titles of Rājādhirāja and Paramēshvara; and with a small cavalry defeated the great Karṇāṭik army, which had won a victory over the kings of the Kānchī, Kērala, Chōla and Pāṇḍya as well as over king Harsha of Kanauj and Vajraṭa.

The Karṇātik army here referred to was the army of the Chālukyas.[4]

1 Indian Antiquary, Vol. XI, page 111.

2 In the copper plate of Talēgāon the reading is "..जेयमन्यैः"

3 This shows that he had conquered Māhīkāṇṭhā, Mālwā and Orissa.

4 The Aihole inscription contains:—

अपरिमितविभूतिस्फीतसामंतसेना-
मणिमुकुटमयूखाक्रान्तपादारविन्दः ।
युधि पतितगजेन्द्राक्रान्तबीभत्सभूतो
भयविगलितहर्षो येन चाकारि हर्षः ॥

i.e., the Chālukya king Pulakēshin II defeated king Harsha of the Vaisa dynasty.

While conquering the Deccan he also defeated the king of Shrī Shaila (in the Karnūl district of Madras).

Similarly, he won victories over the kings of Kalinga,[1] Kōshala,[2] Mālava, Lāṭa[3] and Ṭanka, as well as over the Shēshas (Nāgas). At Ujjain he distributed a large quantity of gold in charity and dedicated jewelled helmets to the God 'Mahākālēshvara.' This indicates that he was a great king of the South. His mother granted lands in charity in almost all the (4,00,000) villages of his kingdom.

A copper grant,[4] of Shaka S. 679 (V.S. 814=A.D. 757), found at Vakkalērī, indicates that though Dantidurga had seized the kingdom from Sōlankī (Chālukya) Kīrtivarman II, before Shaka S. 675 (V.S. 810=A.D. 753), yet the latter had retained possession of its southern part upto Shaka S. 679 (V.S. 814=A.D. 757).

A copper grant[5] of Shaka S. 679(V.S. 814=A.D. 757), of Mahārājādhirāja Karkarāja II of Gujrat, found in the neighbourhood of Sūrat, shows that this Dantivarman (Dantidurga II), at the time of his victory over the Sōlankīs, had also conquered Lāṭa (Gujrat) and made it over to his relative Karkarāja[6] II.

We come across two names of this king—Dantivarman and Dantidurga. The following appear to be his titles:—Mahārājādhirāja, Paramēshvara, Parama Bhaṭṭāraka, Prithvīvallabha, Vallabharāja, Mahārāja Sharva, Khaḍgāvalōka, Sāhasatunga, Vairamēgha.

---

1 The country near the sea-coast between the Mahānadī and the Gōdāvarī.

2 This refers to southern Kōshala (or the modern Central Provinces) which was to the south of the province of Oudh, as the province containing Ayōdhyā and Lucknow, etc., was then called northern Kōshala.

3 Country west of the Narmadā near the modern Baroda State.

4 Epigraphia Indica, Vol. V, page 202.

5 Journal Bombay Asiatic Society, Vol. XVI, page 106.

6 The ruler of Gujrāt at that time was Gurjara Jayabhaṭṭa III, as appears from his copper grant of Chēdī S. 486 (V.S. 793=A.D. 736). Soon after this Dantidurga II probably seized it from him and made it over to Karkarāja.

The title 'Khaḍgāvalōka' probably implies that his look had the terrible effect of a sword on his enemies.

From the above facts, it is evident that Dantidurga was a very powerful king and his dominions extended from the northern borders of Gujrat and Mālwā to Rāmēshvaram in the south.[1]

It appears that after taking the small principalities of the neighbourhood, Dantidurga conquered the Central Provinces. On his return he again went to Kānchī, for the king of that place had, once again, made a fruitless attempt to regain his lost freedom.[2]

In the aforesaid Dashāvatāra inscription, Dantidurga is stated to have defeated Sandhu Bhūpādhipa, whose kingdom probably was in the south somewhere near Kānchī as the inscription mentions, "Kānchī" just after this event.

7. KRISHṆARĀJA I.

He was the younger brother of Indrarāja II and uncle of Dantidurga whom he succeeded.

Three stone inscriptions and one copper grant of the reign of this king have been found:—The first inscription, bearing no date, was found at Hattimattūr.[3] The second of Shaka S. 690 (V.S. 825=A.D. 768) at Talēgāon; and the third of Shaka S. 692 (V.S. 827=A.D. 770) at Ālās.[4]

The copper grant of his reign is dated Shaka S. 694 (V.S. 829=A.D. 772.)[5]

---

1 In the copper grant of Rāshṭrakūṭa Gōvindarāja, found from Paiṭhan (Nizam's Dominions), it is stated that he had extended his sway all over India from Rāmēshvaram in the south to the Himālayas in the north and from the Western Coast to the Eastern Coast.

2 In the inscription, of Shaka S. 836 (V.S. 971), of Nausārī, it is thus stated:—

"काञ्चीपदे पदमकारि करेण भूयः"

Epigraphia Indica, Vol. IX, page 21.

3 Epigraphia Indica, Vol. VI, page 161.

4 Do. do. do. page 209. (This inscription belongs to his—Krishṇarāja's—son, prince regent Gōvindarāja.)

5 Epigraphia Indica, Vol. XIV, page 125.

A copper grant,[1] of Shaka S. 730 (V.S. 864=A.D. 807), of the Rāshṭrakūṭa king Gōvindarāja III, found at Vāṇīgāon (Nāsik), alludes to Krishṇarāja as follows:—

यश्चालुक्यकुलादनूनविबुधव्राताश्रयो वारिधे-
र्लक्ष्मीम्मन्दरवत्सलीलमचिरादाकृष्टवान् वल्लभः ॥

i.e., just as at the time of churning the sea the 'Mandarāchala' mountain had drawn out Lakshmī from it; in like manner, Vallabha (Krishṇarāja I) drew out Lakshmī, *i.e.*, seized the kingdom from the Sōlankī (Chālukya dynasty).

Another copper grant,[2] of Shaka S. 734 (V. S. 869=A.D. 812), of the Rāshṭrakūṭa king Karkarāja of Gujrāt, found at Barōdā, refers to this king Krishṇa I in the following terms:—

योयुद्धकण्डूतिगृहीतमुच्चैः शौर्योष्मसंदीपितमापतन्तम् ।
महावराहं हरिणीचकार प्राज्यप्रभावः खलु राजसिंहः ॥

i.e., Khrishṇarāja I, the lion (most powerful) among kings, turned the great boar (Kīrtivarman II), proudly advancing to fight, into a deer (*i.e.*, put him to flight).

This event probably took place about V. S. 814 (A.D. 757).

As the copper grants of the Sōlankīs bear the mark of a boar, the poet has aptly compared king Kīrtivarman to a boar.

We also understand from this that in the time of Krishṇarāja I, the Sōlankī king Kīrtivarman II had made an attempt to regain his kingdom but, far from achieving any success, he even lost what had remained in his possession.

The army of the king Krishṇa also included a large cavalry.

It was this king, who got the Shiva temple known as "Kailāsa Bhavna" built in the famous Ēlōra caves, in the Nizam's dominions. This temple is made by

1 Indian Antiquary, Vol. XI, page 157.

2 Indian Antiquary, Vol. XII, page 159.

cutting into the rock and is famed for its architecture. Here he also constructed a 'Dēvakula' known after him as "Kannēshvara" where many scholars used to live. Besides this he built 18 other Shiva temples which testifies that he was a staunch Shaiva.

The following were the titles of this king:—

Akālavarsha, Shubhatunga, Prithvīvallabha and Shrīvallabha.

He also defeated the self-conceited king Rāhappa.[1] Vincent Smith and other scholars are of opinion that this Krishṇa I had usurped the kingdom by ousting his nephew Dantidurga II.[2] But this view is incorrect, as from the words 'तस्मिन् दिवंगते' (*i.e.*, on the demise of Dantidurga) occurring in the copper grants[3] found at Kāvī and Navasārī, it is evident that Krishṇa had ascended the throne on the death of his nephew Dantidurga.

From the aforesaid grant[4] found at Barōdā it appears that during the reign of this king a prince of this branch of the Rāshṭrakūṭas had made an attempt to usurp the kingdom. But Krishṇarāja subdued him.[5] It is probable that this prince was a son of Dantidurga II and that Krishṇarāja might have assumed power owing to his minority or weakness.

Though it is clearly stated in the copper grant of Karkarāja (dated Shaka S. 894) found at Kardā[6] that

---

1 Epigraphia Indica, Vol. III, page 105. Some scholars consider this Rāhappa to be second name of Karkarāja II of Gujrāt. It is possible that the rule of Gujrāt branch of the Rāshṭrakūṭas might have thus met its end.

2 Oxford history of India, page 216.

3 Indian Antiquary, Vol. V, page 146; and Journal Bombay Asiatic Society, Vol. XVIII, page 257.

4 Journal Bengal Asiatic Society, Vol. VIII, pages 292-93.

5 यो वंश्यमुन्मूल्य विमार्गभाजं राज्यं स्वयं गोत्रहिताय चक्रे ।

Some scholars identify this event with the dispossession of Karkarāja II of his kingdom of Gujrāt. It is probable that Karkarāja might have raised some disturbance on the death of Dantidurga II

6 Indian Antiquary, Vol. XII, page 264.

Krishṇa uncle of Dantidurga II succeeded to the throne on the latter dying issueless, yet, as the inscription is dated about 200 years after this event, it is to be relied on with caution.

Krishṇarāja I might have acended the throne about V. S. 817 (A.D. 760). He had two sons, Gōvindarāja and Dhruvarāja.

Some scholars hold this Krishṇarāja I, to be the hero of Halayudha's 'Kavirahasya,[1] while others think that the poem treats of Krisṇarāja III. The latter opinion seems correct. The following is an extract from the work:—

अस्त्यगस्त्यमुनिज्योत्स्नापवित्रे दक्षिणापथे ।
कृष्णराज इति ख्यातो राजा साम्राज्यदीक्षितः ॥
....
कस्तं तुलयति स्थाम्ना राष्ट्रकूटकुलोद्भवम् ।
....
सोमं सुनोति यज्ञेषु सोमवंशविभूषणः ।
पुरः सुवति संग्रामे स्यन्दनं स्वयमेव सः ॥

i.e., in southern India there is a great king named Krishṇarāja.......No other king is a match for this Rāshṭrakūṭa king.........This 'Chandravamshī' king performs various sacrifices and keeps his chariot foremost on battle-fields.

The famous Jain logician Akalanka Bhaṭṭa, the author of 'Rājavārtika', and other works flourished in his reign.

SILVER COINS.

About 1800 silver coins of Rāshṭrakūṭa king Krishṇa-rāja were found at Dhamōrī (Amrāotī, Berār district). These coins are similar to those of the Satraps. They are equal in size to the British Indian silver two annas piece, but in thickness they are about double of it. On the obverse there is the king's head while on the reverse there is an inscription as below:—

" परममाहेश्वरमहादित्यपादानुध्यात श्रीकृष्णराज "

1 The followers of this opinion consider the date of compilation of the 'Kavirahasya' as V. S. 867 (A.D. 810).

8. GŌVINDARĀJA II.

He was the son and successor of Krishṇarāja I. From his aforesaid[1] copper grant of Shaka S. 692 (V.S. 827=A.D. 770) it appears that he had conquered Vēngī[2] (the eastern coast district between the Gōdāvarī and the Krishṇā). He is mentioned as prince in this plate; which shows that his father Krishṇarāja I was alive till then.

Two more copper grants of his time are found. The first of these is of Shaka S. 697[3] (V.S. 832=A.D. 775), in which the name of his younger brother Dhruvarāja appears with the titles—Mahārājādhirāja, etc. The second is of Shaka S. 701[4] (V.S. 836=A.D. 779) from which it appears that Gōvindarāja was the king even at that time. In this plate the name of Dhruvarāja's son is mentioned as Karkarāja. From these two copper grants we infer that at that time Gōvinda was a king in name only.

As Gōvindarāja's name does not occur in the copper grants of Vāṇīdindōrī, Barōdā and Rādhanpur, we understand that his younger brother Dhruvarāja had probably dispossessed him of the kingdom. From the copper grant of Wardhā we learn that this Gōvindarāja II was addicted to women and had entrusted the government to his younger brother Nirupama.[5] Probably this vice had caused his downfall.

---

1 Epigraphia Indica, Vol. VI, page 209.

2 He had gained this victory during his father's life time. When his camp was pitched near the confluence of the river Krishṇā, Vēnā and Musī, the king of Vēngi approached him and acknowldged his supremacy.

3 Epigraphia Indica, Vol. X, page 86.

4 Do. do. VIII, page 184.

5 गोविन्दराज इति तस्य बभूव नाम्ना सूनुः सभोगभरभंगुरराज्यचिन्तः ।
आत्मानुजे निरुपमे विनिवेश्य सम्यक् साम्राज्यमीश्वरपदं शिथिलीचकार ॥

i.e., king Gōvinda II, son of Krishṇarāja I, being addicted to love of women, entrusted the work of his government to his younger brother Nirupama whereby his power declined.

From the copper grant,[1] found at Paiṭhan, it appears that Gōvindarāja II had again made an attempt, with the assistance of the neighbouring kings of Mālwā, Kānchī, Vēngi, etc., to regain his lost power, but his younger brother Nirupama (Dhruvarāja) defeated him and brought the kingdom under his complete sway.

The jain author Jinasēna of the 'Digambara' sect, at the close of his work 'Harivamsha Purāṇa.' has stated as follows:—

शाकेष्वब्दशतेषु सप्तसु दिशं पञ्चोत्तरेषूत्तरां
पातीन्द्रायुधनाम्नि कृष्णनृपजे श्रीवल्लभे दक्षिणाम् ।
पूर्वां श्रीमदवन्तिभूभृति नृपे वत्सादि (धि) राजेऽपरां
सोर्या (रा) णामधिमण्डलं (लं) जययुते वीरे वराहेऽवति ॥

i.e., in Shaka S. 705 (V.S. 840=A.D. 783), when this book (Purāṇa) was written, king Indrāyudha[2] reigned in the north; Krishṇa's son, Shrīvallabha in the south; Vatsrāja of 'Avantī' in the east; and Varāha in the west.

From this we conclude that upto Shaka S. 705 (V.S. 840) Gōvindarāja II[3] was ruling, because we learn from the grants of Paiṭhan[4] and Paṭṭadakal[5] that his title was "Vallabha" while that of his younger brother, Dhruvarāja "Kalivallabha."

The following were also the titles of Gōvinda II:—

Mahārājādhirāja, Prabhūtavarsha, and Vikramāvalōka. The date of his succession should be about V.S. 832 (A.D. 775), because there exists an inscription of Shaka S. 694 (V.S. 829=A.D. 772) of his father Krishṇarāja I.

---

1 Epigraphia Indica, Vol. IV, page 107.

2 Some scholars consider this Indrāyudha to be Rāshṭrakūṭa king of Kanauj. Defeating his successor Chakrāyudh, Pratihāra Nāgabhaṭa II, son of Vatsarāja seized the kingdom of Kanauj.

3 Some scholars hold that the Shrīvallabha mentioned here was Gōvindarāja III, but it is not acceptable.

4 Epigraphia Indica, Vol. III, page 105.

5 Indian Antiquary, Vol. XI, page 125. (This inscription belongs to the reign of Dhruvarāja.)

9. DHRUVARĀJA.

He was the son of Krishṇarāja I and the younger brother of Gōvindarāja II. He dethroned his elder brother Gōvinda II and usurped the throne.

He was a brave and wise ruler as his title Nirupama denotes. He defeated the Pallava king of Kānchī from whom he took some elephants as a fine. He imprisoned the king of Chēra of the Ganga dynasty, attacked Pratihāra Vatsarāja,[1] the ruler of the North and conqueror of Gauḍa, seized from him the two canopies that he had obtained from the king of Gauḍa, and drove him towards Bhīnmāl (Marwar).

It is this Vatsarāja who is mentioned in stanza of the 'Harivamsha Purāṇa', quoted above in the history of Gōvindarāja II.

We learn from the copper grant of Begumra[2] that this Dhruvarāja had also seized a canopy from the king of northern Kōshala. The copper grant[3] of Deoli (Wardhā) also supports this view, in which Dhruvarāja is stated to have got three white canopies, two of which were those seized from Vatsarāja and the third must have been taken from the king of Kōshala.

In all probability the kingdom of Dhruvarāja extended over the country from Ayōdhyā in the north to Rāmēshvaram in the south.

In the history of his elder brother Gōvindarāja we have taken notice of two copper grants of Shaka S. 697 and 701. These plates, properly speaking, pertain to this king.

Three inscriptions[4] in Canarese have been found

---

1 When Vatsarāja invaded Malwa, Dhruvarāja went with his feudatory, Rāshṭrakūṭa Karkarāja, the ruler of Lāṭa (Gujrāt), to the help of the king of Malwa. In this action Vatsarāja being deafeated escaped towards Bhīnmāl.

2 J. Bombay Asiatic Society, Vol. XVIII, page 261.

3 Indian Antiquary, Vol. V, page 192.

4 Indian Antiquary, Vol. XI, page 125; and Epigraphia Indica, Vol. VI, pages 163 and 166.

at Paṭṭadakal, Narēgal and Lakshmēshvar, which probably also belong to this king.

The following were the titles of Dhruvarāja:—Kalivallabha, Nirupama, Dhārāvarsha, Shrīvallabha, Mahārājādhirāja, Paramēshvara, etc.

In the Narēgal grant he is also mentioned as 'Dōra' (Dhōra) which is a 'Prākrita' form of his name.

Another broken inscription[1] in Canārese has been found at Shravaṇa Bēlgōlā which is of the time of Mahāsāmantādhipati Kambayya (Stambha) Raṇāvalōka. This Raṇāvalōka is mentioned (in this inscription) as the son of Shrīvallabha.

The date of the accession of Dhruvarāja should be about V.S. 842 (A.D. 785).[2]

When he usurped the kingdom of his elder brother Gōvindarāja II, the kings of Ganga, Vēngi,[3] Kānchī, and Mālwā sided with him (Gōvinda II) but Dhruvarāja defeated them all. He appointed in his life-time his son Gōvindarāja III as the ruler of the country from Kanṭhikā (Konkan) to Khambhāt (Cambay).

In the copper plate[4] dated Shaka S. 715 (V.S. 850= A.D. 793), found at Daulatābād, there is a mention of the charity given by prince Shankaragaṇa, uncle of Dhruvarāja and son of Nanna (grandson of Karkarāja). This inscription also shows that Dhruvarāja was ruling at that time and that he had assumed the sovereignty to save the kingdom of the Rāshṭrakūṭas from the covetous neighbours who tried to take advantage of the weakness of Gōvindarāja II.

---

1 Inscriptions at Shravaṇa Bēlgōlā, Vol. 24, page 3.

2 Vincent Smith holds A.D. 780 as the date of the accession of this king.

3 The king of Vēngi at the time probably was Vishṇuvardhana IV of the Eastern Chālukya dynasty.

4 Epigraphia Indica, Vol. IX, page 193.

10. GŌVINDARĀJA III.

He was the son and successor of Dhruvarāja. Though he had other brothers, his father, finding him the ablest of all, intended in his life-time to invest him with the ruling powers but he disapproved of the proposal and carried on the administration as a prince regent during his father's life-time.

His titles appear to be:—"Prithvīvallabha, Pabhūtavarsha, Shrīvallabha, Vimalāditya, Jagattunga, Kīrtinārāyaṇa,[1] Atishayadhavala, Tribhuvanadhavala, and Janavallabha, etc. Nine copper grants have been found of his time. The first[2] is of Shaka S. 716 (V.S. 851=A.D. 794) found at Paiṭhan. The second[3] is of Shaka S. 726 (V. S. 861=A. D. 804) found at Somēshvara, which discloses that his queen's name was "Gāmuṇḍabbē" and that he defeated king Dantiga of Kānchī (Kānjivaram).

This Dantiga might be the Dantivarman of the Pallava dynasty whose son Nandivarman married princess Shankhā, the daughter of the Rāshṭrakūṭa king Amōghavarsha.

The third and the fourth plates[4] are of Shaka S. 730 (V.S. 865=A.D. 808). From these we learn that Gōvindarāja had defeated the combined armies of 12 kings assembled under the banner of his brother Stambha.[5] (This shows that on the death of Dhruvarāja,

1 The inscription dated Shaka S. 788 (V. S. 923=A.D. 866) of his son Amōghavarsha I, found at Nilgund, indicates that Gōvindarāja III was called Kīrtinārāyaṇa, as he fettered the people of Kērala, Mālava, Gauḍa, Gurjara and those living in the hillfort of Chitrakūṭa and subdued the Lord of Kānchī.

(Epigraphia Indica, Vol. V, page 102).

2 Do. do. Vol. III, page 105.

3 Indian Antiquary, Vol. XI, page 126.

4 Indian Antiquary, Vol. XI, page 157; and Epigraphia Indica, Vol. VI, page 242.

5 In the copper grant of Shaka S. 724 of Stambha, found at Nēlmangal, the name Shauchakhambha (Shauchakambha) is stated instead of Stambha —

"भ्राताभूत्तस्य शक्तित्रयनमितभुवः शौचखम्भाभिधानो"

From this copper grant it also appears that after this defeat Shauchakhambha may have remained obedient to king Gōvindarāja. Another name of this Shaucha-

Stambha may have made an attempt, with the assistance of the neighbouring kings, to usurp the kingdom.)

Gōvindarāja liberated king Ganga of Chēra (Coimbatur) who was taken prisoner by his father (Dhruvarāja). But when Ganga again prepared to rebel, he recaptured and re-imprisoned him. From these copper grants we also learn that this Gōvindarāja III, having attacked the king of Gujrāt, had put him to flight and conquered Mālwā. He, having subjected Mārāsharva on his invasion of Vindhyāchala, kept his residence at Shrī Bhavana (Malkhed) till the end of the rains and at the advent of the winter advanced towards the Tungabhadrā (river) and defeated the Pallava king of Kānchī. Later, in obedience to his call, the king of Vēngi, (country between the Krishṇā and the Gōdāvarī) probably Vijayāditya II of the Eastern Chālukya dynasty, attended his court and acknowledged his supremacy.

From the copper grant[1] of Sanjān we learn that Dharmāyudha and Chakrayudha also acknowledged his supremacy.

The kings of Banga and Magadha also yielded to him.

As his expedition upto the Tungabhadrā is noted in the copper grant of Shaka S. 726, it appears that all these events had taken place before this date (*i.e.*, V. S. 861=A.D. 804).

The said third and fourth copper grants were found at Wāṇī and Rādhanpur and indicate that they were inscribed at Muyūrakhandī, the modern Mōrkhand in the Nāsik district.

The fifth and sixth plates are of Shaka S. 732

khambha was Raṇāvalōka. At the recommendation of prince Bappaya he made a grant of a village for a Jain temple (Epigraphii Carnāṭica, maṇṇe grant, No. 61, p. 51).

1 Unpublished grant.

(V.S. 867=A.D. 810), and the seventh[1] is of Shaka S. 733 (V.S. 868=A.D. 811).

The eighth[2] plate is of Shaka S. 734 (V.S. 869=A.D. 812); it contains a mention of the charitable grant made by king Karkarāja of Gujrāt.

The ninth[3] plate of Shaka S. 735 (V.S. 870=A.D. 813) shows that this Gōvindarāja III, having conquered Lāṭa[4] (the central and southern part of Gujrāt), had made his younger brother Indrarāja the ruler of that territory. This Indrarāja was the founder of the second branch of the Rāshṭrakūṭa kings of Gujrāt.

From the aforesaid facts it appears that this Gōvindarāja III was a powerful monarch. Kings of the countries between the Vindhya and Mālwā in the north to Kānchī in the south were under his sway, and his own kingdom extended from the Narmadā to the Tungabhadrā.

One more copper grant[5] of Shaka S. 735 (V.S. 870=A.D. 813) has been found at Kadamba (Mysore) which contains a mention of a charitable grant made to the Jain priest Arkakīrti, the disciple of Vijayakīrti. This Vijayakīrti was a disciple of Kulāchārya and this grant was made on the recommendation of king Chākirāja of the Ganga dynasty.

In the date of this plate Monday is mentioned as the corresponding day, whereas by calculation Friday falls on that date. Thus, there is some doubt about the genuineness of this plate.

In the foregoing history of Gōvindarāja II, we have cited a stanza from the 'Harivamshapurāṇa.' Its second line reads as follows:—

---

1 Watson Museum Report, for 1925-26, page 13.

2 Indian Antiquary, Vol. XII, page 156.

3 Epigraphia Indica, Vol. III, page 54.

4 The country between the Tāptī and the Māhī rivers.

5 Indian Antiquary, Vol. XII, page 13 and Epigraphia Indica, Vol. IV, page 340.

"पातीन्द्रायुधनाम्नि कृष्णनृपजे श्रीवल्लभे दक्षिणाम्" Some scholars consider the phrase 'कृष्णनृपजे' here to be connected with 'श्रीवल्लभे' while others think it to be going with the preceding name 'इन्द्रायुध'.

According to the first reading Gōvinda II is meant here as the king of the Deccan, while according to the second reading, if we take Indrāyudha to be the son of Krishṇarāja, then the word "Shrīvallabha" remains alone. Thus, those who favour the latter opinion hold that Gōvinda III, and not Gōvinda II, was ruling in Shaka S. 705; but this is not acceptable.

In an inscription[1] of Shaka S. 788 (V.S. 923-A.D. 866), found at Nilgund, it is stated that this Gōvinda III had conquered Kērala, Mālava, Gurjara and Chitrakūṭa (Chittor). His date of accession ought to be just after V.S. 850 (A.D. 973). The Eastern Chālukya king of Vēngi had to build a city wall around Mānyakhēṭa for its protection, by way of subsidy.

In an inscription[2] found at Monghyr, it is stated that Raṇṇādēv,ī the daughter of the Rāshṭrakūṭa king Prabala[3], was married to king Dharmapāla of the Pāla dynasty of Bengal. Dr. Kielhorn holds this Parbaḷa to be king Gōvinda III, but Sir Bhandārkar identifies him with Krishṇa II.[4]

11. AMŌGHAVARSHA I.

He was the son and successor of Gōvinda III. The real name of this king has not yet been known. Perhaps, it was "Sharva," but in the copper plates, etc., he is named as Amōghavarsha, *e.g.* :—

स्वेच्छागृहीतविषयान् दृढसंगभाजः
प्रोद्वृत्तदृप्ततरशौल्किकराष्ट्रकूटान् ।
उत्खातखड्गनिजबाहुबलेन जित्वा
योऽमोघवर्षमचिरात्स्वपदे व्यधत्त ॥

1 Epigraphia Indica, Vol. VI page 102.
2 Indian Antiquary, Vol. XXI, page 254.
3 See pages 48-49.
4 Bhārata-kē-Prāchīna Rājavamsha, Vol. I, page 185,

i. e., he (Karkarāja) installed Amōghavarsha on the throne by putting down the Rāshṭrakūṭas, that had revolted and seized the territories.

But in fact Amōghavarsha seems to be only the title of the king. The following titles of this king have also been found:—Nripatunga, Mahārāja Sharva, Mahārāja Shaṇḍa, Atishayadhavala, Vīra Nārāyaṇa, Prithvīvallabha, Shrī Prithvīvallabha, Lakshmīvallabha, Mahārājādhirāja, Bhaṭāra, Parama Baṭṭāraka, Prabhūtavarsha, and Jagattunga.

He possessed the following seven emblems of the state:—Three white canopies, one conch, one 'Pālidhvaja,' one 'Ōkakētu' and one 'Trivalī'. The three white canopies mentioned here are, perhaps, the same that were acquired by Gōvinda II.

The following are the copper grants and the inscriptions of the time of this king:—

The first copper grant,[1] of Shaka S. 738 (V.S. 873=A.D. 817), of Rāshṭrakūṭa king Karkarāja of Gujrāt was found at Barōdā. This Karkarāja was the cousin of Amōghavarsha. The second copper plate,[2] of Shaka S. 749 (V.S. 884=A.D. 827), was found at Kāvī (Broach district); it speaks of the charity distributed by the Rāshṭrakūṭa king Gōvindarāja of Gujrāt.

The third plate,[3] of Shaka S. 757 (V.S. 892=A.D. 835), of Mahāsāmantādhipati, Rāshṭrakūṭa king Dhruvarāja[4] I of Gujrāt, found at Barōdā, shows that the name of Amōghavarsha's uncle was Indrarāja and that his son (Amōghavarsha's cousin) Karkarāja subduing the rebellious Rāshṭrakūṭas placed Amōghavarsha on the throne.

---

1 Journal Bombay Branch Asiatic Society, Vol. XX, page 135.

2 Indian Antiquary, Vol. V, page 144.

3 Indian Antiquary, Vol. XIV, page 199.

4 Some scholars are of opinion that Dhruvarāja I, of Lāṭa (Gujrāt), had made a futile attempt on Amōghavarsha, who was therefore obliged to march against him. Probably Dhruvarāja was killed in this action.

The first inscription,[1] of Shaka S. 765 (V.S. 900-A.D. 843), fixed in a cave at Kanhērī (in the Thānā district), shows that Amōghavarsha was ruling in that year, and that his chief feudatory Pulla Shakti (the successor of Kapardipāda) was the governor of the whole of the Kōnkan district. The Pulla Shakti belonged to the Shilāhāra dynasty of the northern Kōnkan.

The second inscription,[2] of Shaka S. 775 (V.S. 910-A.D. 853), of Kapardi II, the successor of Pulla Shakti, the chief feudatory, is fixed in another cave at Kaṇhērī. Scholars suppose the actual date of this inscription to be Shaka S. 773 (V.S. 908-A.D. 851). This also shows that Pulla Shakti was a Buddhist.

The third inscription,[3] of Shaka S. 782 (V.S. 917=A.D. 860), of Amōghavarsha himself, found at Kōnūr, contains a mention of the charity granted by him to the Jain priest Dēvēndra at his capital city Mānyakhēṭa. In this plate, the Rāshṭrakūṭas are stated to be the off shoots of Yadu, and a new title "Vīra Nārāyaṇa" of king Amōghavarsha is also found in it.

As he had granted lands in 30 villages for a Jain temple built by Bankēya,[4] it appears that he patronised Jainism.

---

1 Indian Antiquary, Vol. XIII, page 136.

2 Do. do. XIII, page 134.

3 Epigraphia Indica, Vol. VI, page 29.

4 This Bankēya belonged to the Mukula clan and was a governor of 30,000 villages under Amōghavarsha. He by the command of the latter invaded Vaṭāṭavī of Gangavāḍī. Though the other feudatories refused to help him he advanced and took possession of the fort of Kēḍal (north-west of Kaḍav). Proceeding further, he defeated the ruler of Talavan (Talkāḍ on the left bank of the Kāvērī) and crossing the Kāvērī, he invaded the province of Saptapada In the meantime, the son of Amōghavarsha raised the banner of rebellion and many feudatories joined him. But on the return of Bankēya the prince fled away and his allies were all killed. Pleased with this service Amōghavarsha granted the said lands for the Jain temple built by him.

This copper plate speaks of a rebellion by the prince; but in the unpublished copper plate of Shaka S. 793 of Sanjān the word 'पुत्रश्चास्माकमेक:'—(श्लोक १६) shows that Amōghavarsha had only one son (whom he invested with the ruling powers during his life-time).

The fourth inscription,[1] of Shaka S. 787 (V.S. 922=A.D. 865), of the time of this king, has been found at Mantravāḍī, the fifth[2] of Shaka S. 788 (V.S. 923=A.D. 866) at Shirūr and the sixth[3] (of the same date) at Nīlgunḍ; all these belong to the 52nd year of his reign.

From the aforesaid Shirur inscription it appears that Amōghavarsha's coat-of-arms bore an image of 'Garuḍa,'[4] that his title was 'Laṭalūrādhīshvara', and that the kings of Anga, Banga, Magadha, Mālava, and Vēngi acknowledged his superiority. Probably, there may be some exaggeration in this statement.

The seventh inscription[5] of hisfeudatory Bankēyarasa has been found at Niḍgunḍī, which is of the 61st year of Amōghavarsha's reign. In the fourth unpublished copper grant of Shaka S. 793 (V.S. 928=A.D. 871), found at Sanjān, it is stated that Amōghavarsha had made great efforts to overthrow the kingdom of the Draviḍas; that the mobilisation of his armies struck terror in the hearts of the kings of Kēral, Pānḍya, Chōla, Kalinga, Magadha, Gujrāt and Pallava; and that he had imprisoned for life the 'Gangavamshī' ruler and those dependants of his own court who had carried on intrigues with him.

The king[6] of Vēngi got constructed a wall around his garden.

The fifth copper grant[7], of Shaka S. 789 (V.S. 924=A.D. 867), of the chief feudatory Dhruvarāja

1 Epigraphia Indica, Vol. VII, page 198.

2 Epigraphia Indica, Vol. VII, page 203; Indian Antiquary, Vol. XII, page 218.

3 Epigraphia Indica, Vol. VI, page 102.

4 This shows that he was a follower of Vaishṇavism.

5 Epigraphia Indica, Vol. VII, page 212.

6 Later as this king of Vēngi oppressed his subjects, Amōghavarsha imprisoned him and his minister, and, to give publicity to their misdeeds erected their statues in the 'Shiva' temple at Kānchī.

7 Indian Antiquary, Vol. XII, page 181.

II[1] of Gujrāt, contains a mention of a charitable grant made by him (Dhruvarāja).

The eighth inscription[2] of Shaka S. 799 (V.S. 934= A.D. 877), fixed in a cave at Kaṇhērī, shows that king Amōghavarsha, being pleased with his feudatory Kapardī II, of the Shilārī clan, made over to him the kingdom of the whole of Kōnkan. From this inscription it also appears that Buddhism had survived in India till then.

From the aforesaid copper grant of Shaka S. 757 (V.S. 892), of Dhruvarāja I of Gujrāt, it appears that some disturbances had arisen at the time of Amōghavarsha's accession, when his cousin Karkarāja had helped him. But from the contents of the subsequent inscriptions we understand that Amōghavarsha had gradually gained great power. He shifted his capital from Nāsik to Mānyakhēṭa (Malkhēd),[3] and remained at constant war[4] with the western Chālukyas of Vēngi.

---

1. Perhaps a war took place between this Dhruvarāja II of Gujrāt and Amōghavarsha I.

2 Indian Antiquary, Vol. XIII, page 135.

3 This Malkhēḍ exists even today about 90 miles to the south-east of Sholapur in the Nizam's dominions.

4 The copper grant of Vijayāditya contains the following :—

गंगारट्टबलैःसार्धं द्वादशाब्दानहर्निशं ॥
भुजार्जितबलः खड्गसहायो नवविक्रमैः ।
अष्टोत्तरं युद्धशतं युद्ध्वा शंभोर्महालयम् ॥
तत्संख्यमकरोद्धीरो विजयादित्यभूपतिः ।

i.e., in 12 years Vijayāditya II fought 108 battles with the kings of the Rāshṭrakūṭa and the Ganga dynasties, and later built an equal number of 'Shiva' temples. This shows that internal discord may have afforded an opportunity to Vijayāditya to attack and probably to take some portion of the territory of the Rāshṭrakūṭas, which Amōghavarsha eventually recaptured, as appears from the following stanza in the copper grant of Navasārī :—

निमग्नां यश्चलुक्याब्धौ रट्टराज्यश्रियं पुनः ।
पृथ्वीमिवोद्धरन् धीरो वीरनारायणोऽभवत् ॥

i.e., just as Varāha (one of the incarnations of God) had delivered the earth that had been submerged in the sea, in the like manner, Amōghavarsha delivered once again the kingdom of the Rāshṭrakūṭas that had lapsed under the surging sea of the Chālukyas.

A copper grant[1] of the western Ganga dynasty, found at Sūndī, shows that Amōghavarsha had a daughter named Abbalabbā who was married to 'Guṇadattaranga Bhūtuga,' the great grandfather of 'Pēramānaḍī Bhūtuga.' This 'Pēramānaḍī' was a feudatory of the Rāshṭrakūṭa king Krishṇa III. But this plate is held by scholars to be a forged one.

According to the aforesaid inscription of Shaka S. 788, the date of the accession of this king comes about Shaka S. 736 (V.S. 871-A.D. 815).

The latter part of the 'Mahāpurāṇa' written by Guṇabhadra sūri (and known as Uttara purāṇa) contains the following:—

यस्य प्रांशुनखांशुजालविसरद्धारान्तराविर्भव-
त्पादाम्भोजरजः पिशङ्गमुकुटप्रत्यग्ररत्नद्युतिः ।
संस्मर्त्ता स्वममोघवर्षनृपतिः पूतोऽहमद्येत्यलं
स श्रीमाञ्जिनसेनपूज्यभगवत्पादो जगन्मङ्गलम् ॥

i.e., blissful for the world is the existence of Jinasēnāchārya, by bowing to whom Amōghavarsha considered himself to be purified.

This shows that Amōghavarsha was a follower of the 'Digambara' branch of Jainism and was a pupil of Jinasēna.[2]

This fact is also borne out by the 'Pārshvābhyudaya Kāvya'[3] written by Jinasēna. The same Jinasēna compiled the Ādipurāṇa (the first half of the Mahāpurāṇa). In the preface to Gaṇitasārasangraha', a book on mathematics written by Mahāvīrāchārya, Amōghavarsha is stated to be the follower of Jainism.

The "Jayadhavalā," a book containing the principles

1 Epigraphia Indica, Vol. III, page 176.

2 This Jinasēna was also the author of the 'Pārshvābhyudaya Kāvya' and belonged to the 'Sēnasangha', while Jinasēna the author of the 'Harivamsha Purāṇa' (written in Shaka S. 705) belonged to the 'Punnāṭa Sangha.'

3 'इत्यमोघवर्षपरमेश्वरपरमगुरुश्रीजिनसेनाचार्यविरचिते मेघदूतवेष्टिते पार्श्वाभ्युदये भगवत्कैवल्यवर्णनं नाम चतुर्थः सर्गः ।'

of the 'Digambar' sect of Jainism, was also written in Shaka S. 759 (V.S. 894=A.D. 837) during the reign of Amōghavarsha.

The Jain priests of the 'Digambar' sect hold that the book named "Prashṇōttararatnamālikā" was written by Amōghavarsha himself, when he, being disgusted with the world, had renounced the affairs of the state in old age, but the Brāhmaṇas allege that the book was written by Shankarāchārya,[1] while the 'Svētāmbara' Jains say that its author was Vimalāchārya.

In the 'Digambara' Jain manuscripts of the above book we find the following couplet:—

विवेकात्त्यक्तराज्येन राज्ञेयं रत्नमालिका

रचितामोघवर्षेण सुधियां सदलंकृतिः ।

i.e., king Amōghavarsha, who has renounced the state, being enlightened by real knowledge, has written this book (Ratnamālikā).

From this we learn that in old age the king having made over the reins of the government to his son[2] passed the remainder of his life in religious meditation.

This book Ratnamālikā was translated into the Tibetan language in which also Amōghavarsha is stated to be its author.

Just about this time many books had been written on Jainism that had then begun to gain a footing.

An inscription,[3] of Vankēyarasa bearing no date, has been found which shows that he was a feudatory of Amōghavarsha and ruler of the districts of Banavāsī,

---

1 From the manuscript copy of the 'Prashṇōttararatnamālikā' preserved in the Government Oriental Manuscripts Library, Madras, we learn that Shankarāchārya was the author of the book in question. (Refer catalogue, edited by Kuppu Swami, Vol. II, part I, C, pages 2640-2641).

2 Besides Krishṇarāja, Amōghavarsha had another son named Duddaya (Smith's Early History of India, page 446, Footnote No. 1.)

3 Epigraphia Indica, Vol. VII, page 212.

Bēlgali, Kunḍargē, Kanḍūr, Purīgēḍē (Lakshmēshvara), etc.

From the Kyāsanūr inscription, bearing no date, it appears that Sankaragaṇḍa, a feudatory of Amōghavarsha, was the governor of Banavāsī.[1]

King Prithvīpati I, son of Shivamāra of the Ganga dynasty, was also a contemporary of king Amōghavarsha.[2]

There is a book on prosody named "Kavirājamārga" in the Canarese language which too is said to have been written by king Amōghavarsha.

12. KRISHṆARĀJA II.

He was the son of Amōghavarsha and acquired the powers of government during his father's life-time.

Four inscriptions and two copper grants of his time have been found.

Out of these copper grants the first[3] found at Baghumra (Barōdā district), of Shaka S. 810 (V.S. 945=A.D. 888), contains a mention of the charitable grant made by the chief feudatory Akālavarsha Krishṇarāja of Gujrāt. But this inscription is held unreliable by scholars.

The first inscription[4] of Shaka S. 822 (V.S. 957=A.D. 900) is found at Nandawāḍige (Bījāpur). In fact, it is of Shaka S. 824 (V.S. 959=A.D. 903).[5] The second inscription,[6] which is also of Shaka S. 822, was found at Ardēshahallī.

The third inscription,[7] of Shaka S. 824 (V.S. 959=A.D. 903), has been found at Mulgund (Dhārwār district.)

1 South Indian inscription, Vol. II, No. 76, page 382.

2 C. Mabel Duff's Chronology of India, page 73.

3 Indian Antiquary, Vol. XIII, pages 65-69.

4 Epigraphia Carnatica, Vol. IX, page 98 and Indian Antiquary, Vol. XII, page 221.

5 Indian Antiquary, Vol. XII, page 221.

6 Epigraphia Carnatica, Vol. IX, No. 42, page 98.

7 Journal Bombay branch Royal Asiatic Society, Vol. X, page 190.

The second copper grant,[1] of Shaka S. 832 (V.S. 967=A.D. 910), found at Kapḍavanja (Khaira district), contains a geneological table of this dynasty from king Krishṇa I to Krishṇa II, and a mention of the village granted by the latter in charity. The name of his chief feudatory, Prachanḍa of the Brahmabaka clan,[2] is also found in it. He ruled over 750 villages, Khēṭaka, Harshapur, and Kāsahrada being the chief among them.

The fourth inscription,[3] of Shaka S. 831 (V.S. 966=A.D. 909), has been found at Aiholē (Bijapur), the actual date of which ought to be Shaka S. 833 (V.S. 968=A.D. 912).

The following were the titles of king Krishṇa=rāja II:-Akālavarsha, Shubhatunga, Mahārājādhirāja, Paramēshvara, Parabhaṭṭāraka, Shrī Prithvīvallabha, and Vallabharāja.

In some places the word 'Vallabha' is found affixed to his name such as 'Krishṇavallabha.' A corrupt form of his name in Canarese is found as "Kannara."

He married a princess named Mahādēvī, the daughter of Haihaya king Kōkkala of Chēdī and younger sister of Shankkuka. This Kōkkala I was the king of Tripuri (Tēnavar).[4]

The wars with the Eastern Chālukyas had continued down to the reign of this Krishṇarāja II.[5]

---

1 Epigraphia Indica, Vol. I, page 53.

2 Krishṇarāja had granted a 'Jāgīr' in Gujrāt to Prachanḍa's father in recognition of his services.

3 Indian Antiquary, Vol. XII, page 222.

4 Bhārata-kē-Prāchīna Rājavamsha, part I, page 40.

5 In the copper plate of king Bhīma II, of the Chālukya dynasty of Vēngi, it is thus stated:—

तत्सूनुर्म्मंगिहननक्रष्णपरदहने विख्यातकीर्तिगुणग विजयादित्यश्चतुश्चत्वारिंशतम्

i.e., king Vijayāditya III who killed king Mangi (son of Vishṇuvardhana V, of the Ganga dynasty), and burnt the capital of king Krishṇarāja II, ruled for 44 years. Probably the Rāshṭrakūṭas had after this taken possession of that country which was later recaptured by king Bhīma I, a nephew of Vijayāditya.

(Indian Antiquary, Vol. XIII, page 213.)

There is an inscription[1] of Shaka S. 797 (V.S. 932=A.D. 875), of Prithvīrāma, the chief feudatory of Krishṇarāja II, who had made a charitable grant of land for a Jain temple at Saundatti. From this inscription it appears that Krishṇa II ascended the throne in Shaka S. 797 (V.S. 932=A.D. 875). But in the foregoing narrative of his father (Amōghavarsha I) we have noted that an inscription of Shaka S. 799 (V.S. 934=A.D. 877) of that king has been found. This shows that in Shaka S. 797 (V.S. 932), or even earlier, king Amōghavarsha I had made over the kingdom to his son Krishṇarāja II. Hence, some feudatories might have commenced to mention his name in their inscriptions even during the lifetime of king Amōghavarsha. We have already mentioned in Amōghavarsha's history that in his old age he, having renounced the affairs of the state, had written the book "Prashṇottraratnamālikā." This, too, supports the above opinion.

Krishṇa II conquered the Āndhra, Banga, Kālinga, and Magadha kingdoms, fought with the kings of Gurjara and Gauḍa, and after overthrowing the Rāshṭrakūṭa kingdom annexed the province of Lāṭa. His kingdom extended from the Cape Commorin to the bank of the Ganges.

In the latter part of the 'Mahāpurāṇa' written by Guṇabhadra, a disciple of Jinasēna, it is thus stated:—

अकालवर्षभूपाले पालयत्यखिलामिलाम् ।

....

शकनृपकालाभ्यन्तर विंशत्यधिकाष्टशतमित ब्दान्ते ।

i. e., the 'Uttarapurāṇa' was concluded in Shaka S. 820 (V.S. 955=A.D. 898), in the reign of king Akālavarsha. Hence, this 'purāṇa' may have been finished in the reign of Krishṇa II. His coronation probably took place about Shaka S. 797 (V.S. 932=A.D. 875). But V. A. Smith holds the date of this event to be A.D. 880 (V.S. 937).

1 Journal Bombay Royal Asiatic Society, Vol. X, page 194.

He perhaps died about Shaka S. 833 (V.S. 986=A.D. 911).

The name of the son of Krishṇa II was Jagattunga II who was married to Lakshmī, the daughter of Raṇavigraha (Shankaragaṇa), the son of king Kōkkala of the Kalachuri (Haihaya) dynasty of Chēdī.

Just as Arjuna, the well-known hero of the Mahābhārata, married the daughter of his maternal uncle Vāsudēva, Pradyumna the daughter of Rukma, and Aniruddha the granddaughter of Rukma, in like manner, in this family of the southern Rāshṭrakūṭa kings Krishṇarāja, etc., married the daughters of their maternal uncles. This custom is still prevalent in the south.

From the copper grant found at Wardhā it appears that this Jagattunga had died in his father's lifetime.[1] Therefore, after Krishṇarāja II, Jagattunga's son Indra ascended the throne.

The fact of the marriage of Jagattunga II to Lakshmī, the daughter of Shankaragaṇa,[2] is borne out by the copper grant of Karḍā. But the same plate speaks of Jagattunga as having married Gōvindāmbā, another daughter of Shankaragaṇa and the mother of Amōghavarsha[3] III (Vaddiga), who might have been a younger brother of Indra. (This copper plate also shows that Jagattunga, having conquered many countries, had extended his father's dominions far and wide, but the history relating to the later period is much confused in this plate.)

---

1 अभूज्जगत्तुङ्ग इति प्रसिद्धस्तदंगजः स्त्रीनयनामृतांशुः ।
अलब्धराज्यः स दिवं विनिन्ये दिव्यांगनाप्रार्थनयेव धात्रा ॥

i.e., the handsome prince Jagattunga being devoted to sexual pleasure predeceased his father. This fact is also borne out by the Sānglī and Navsārī copper plates :—

2 Raṇavigraha might be a title of Shankaragaṇa.

3 In the copper grant found at Karḍā it is thus stated :—

चेद्यां मातुलशंकरगणात्मजायामभूज्जगत्तुंगात् ।
श्रीमानमोघवर्षो गोविन्दाम्बाभिधानायाम् ॥

13. INDRARĀJA III.

He was the son of Jagattunga II, and, owing to the latter's predeceasing his father, succeeded to the throne on the death of his grandfather Krishṇarāja. His mother's name was Lakshmī, and he had married Vījāmbā, the daughter of Ammaṇadēva (Anangadēva), son of Arjuna and grandson of Kōkkala of the Kalachuri (Haihaya) dynasty. The following are the titles of Indra III:—Nityavarsha, Mahārājādhirāja, Paramēshvara, Parama Bhaṭṭāraka, and Shrī Prithvīvallabha.

Two copper grants[1] of his time have been found at Bagumra, both of which are of Shaka S. 836 (V.S. 972-A.D. 915). These show that Indra III had moved down from Mānyakhēṭa to the village of Kurundaka for his coronation. And on its completion, on the 7th day of the bright half of Phālguna, Shaka S. 836 (24th February 915),[2] he made a charitable grant of gold equal in weight to that of his person and also of a village in the province of Lāṭa. (This Kurundaka was situated on the confluence of the rivers Krishṇā and Panchagangā).

Besides these, he granted 20 lac Drammas and restored the 400 villages that had been resumed.

In the aforesaid copper plates the Rāshṭrakūṭas are mentioned as the descendants of Sātyaki and it is also stated that Indra III had laid waste Mēru. Mēru here might stand for Mahōdaya (Kanauj), because in the copper grant of Shaka S. 852, of his son Gōvinda IV, it is stated that he, having led his cavalry across the Yamunā, had laid waste Kanauj. And on that account it came to be called 'Kushasthala' a jungle.

1 Epigraphia Indica, Vol. IX, page 29; and Journal Bombay Asiatic Society, Vol. XVIII, pages 257 and 261

2 V. A. Smith gives A.D. 912 as the date of accession of Indra III. We cannot say that how far it is correct as in this plate is thus stated:—

"शकनृपकालातीत संवत्सर [शते] ष्वष्टसुषट्त्रिंशदुत्तरेषु युवसंवत्सरे फाल्गुनशुद्धसप्तम्यां संपन्ने श्रीपट्ट (ब) न्धोत्सवे" which shows that this event took place in A.D. 915.

An inscription[1] of Shaka S. 838 (V.S. 973-A.D. 916), which was found at Hattimattūra (in the Dhārwār district) contains a mention of Lēndēyaras, the chief feudatory of this king.

When Indra III had laid waste Mēru (Mahōdaya or Kanauj) it was ruled over by the Pratihāra Mahīpāla. Though the former had dispossessed the latter of his kingdom yet he regained its possession. But in this confusion Mahīpāla of Pānchāla lost his western possessions (Saurāshṭra, etc).

Trivikrama Bhaṭṭa, the author of the 'Damyantī Kathā' and the 'Madālasā champū,' flourished in his time. The writer of the copper grant of Shaka S. 836 (V.S. 972), of Kurundaka, was the same Trivikrama Bhaṭṭa, the son of Nēmāditya and father of Bhāskra Bhaṭṭa. This Bhāskara Bhaṭṭa was contemporary of the great Paramāra king Bhōja of Mālwā. The famous astronomer Bhāskarāchārya, author of the 'Siddhānta Shirōmaṇī,' was fifth in descent from this Bhāskara Bhaṭṭā.

Indra III, had two sons:—Amōghavarsha and Gōvinda.

14. AMŌGHAVARSHA II.

He was the eldest son of Indrarāja III and had probably ascended the throne after him.

A copper grant[2] of Shaka S. 919 (V.S. 1054-A.D. 997), of Mahāmanḍalēshvara Aparājita Dēvarāja of the Shilāra dynasty, shows that this Amōghavarsha II died soon after his accession (*i.e.*, if he reigned at all it might be for a year or so only.) The date of his accession might be about V.S. 973 (A.D. 916). The Dēōlī grant[3] of Shaka S. 862 (A.D. 940) supports the fact that Amōghavarsha II succeeded Indrarāja III.

1 Indian Antiquary, Vol. XII, page 224.
2 Epigraphia Indica, Vol. III, page 271.
3 Epigraphia Indica, Vol. V, page 192.

15. GŌVINDARĀJA IV.

He was the son of Indrarāja III and younger brother of Amōghavarsha II. The 'Prākrita' form of his name is found to be 'Gōjjiga.' The following were his titles: —Prabhūtavarsha, Suvarṇavarsha, Nṛipatunga, Vīra Nārāyaṇa, Nityakandarpa, Raṭṭakandarpa, Shashānka, Nṛipatitrinētra, Mahārājādhirāja, Paramēshvara, Parama Bhaṭṭāraka, Sāhasānka, Prithvīvallabha, Vallabhanarēndradēva, Vikrāntanārāyṇa, Gōjjigavallabha, etc.

The wars with the Eastern Chālukyas of Vēngi again broke out in his time, as is evident from the inscriptions[1] of Amma I, and Bhīma III. Two inscriptions and two copper grants of the time of this Gōvinda IV have been found. The first[2] of his inscriptions is of Shaka S. 840 (V.S. 975=A.D. 918) found, at Ḍanḍapur (Dhārwār district), and the second[3] is of Shaka S. 851 (V.S. 987-A.D. 930).

In his first copper grant[4] of Shaka S. 852 (V.S. 987-A.D. 930) he is mentioned as the successor of Mahārājādhirāja Indrarāja III, and a 'Yaduvamshī' (of the lunar origin). The second plate,[5] dated Shaka S. 855 (V.S. 990=A.D. 933), from Sānglī, contains a mention of the lineage, etc., like the first.

From the copper grant of Deōlī (Wardhā) it appears that this king (Gōvinda IV) died at an early age

1 In the copper grants of the Chālukyas it is thus stated about Bhīma III :—

'दराडं गोविन्दराजप्रणाहितमधिकं चोलपं लोलविक्कि

विक्रान्तं युद्धमल्लं घटितगजघटं संनिहत्यैक एव ।'

i.e., Bhīma repulsed the armies of Gōvinda and killed Chōla king Lōlavikkī and Yuddhamalla possessor of mighty elephants, without the help of others. This shows that Gōvinda IV may have made an unsuccessful attack upon Bhīma.

At the time of the succession of Amma I, Gōvinda IV had also attacked him but achieved no success.

2 Indian Antiquary, Vol XII, page 223.

3 Do. do. Vol. XII, page 211, (No. 48).

4 Epigraphia Indica, Vol. VII, page 36.

5 Indian Antiquary, Vol. XII, page 249.

owing to the excess of sexual pleasures.[1] The date of his accession might be V.S. 974 (A.D. 917).

16. BADDIGA (AMŌGHAVARSHA III).

He was the grandson of Krishṇarāja II and son of Jagattunga II (from his wife Gōvindāmbā). He succeeded Gōvinda IV, who died a premature death owing to excess of sexual pleasures.

It is stated in the copper grant[2] of Shaka S. 862 (V.S. 997-A.D. 940), of the Rāshṭrakūṭa king Krishṇa III, found at Deōlī (Wārdhā) :—

राज्यं दधे मदनसौख्यविलासकन्दो गोविन्दराज इति विश्रुतनामधेयः ।१७॥
सोप्यङ्गनानयनपाशनिरुद्धबुद्धिरुन्मार्गसंगविमुखीकृतसर्वसत्वः ।
दोषप्रकोपविषमप्रकृतिश्लथांगः प्रापत् क्षयं सहजतेजसि जातजाड्ये ॥१८।

सामन्तैरथरट्टराज्यमहिमालम्बार्थमभ्यर्थितो
देवेनापि पिनाकिना हरिकुलोल्लासैषिणा प्रेरितः ।
अध्यास्त प्रथमो विवेकिषु जगत्तुंगात्मजोमोघवाक्
पीयूषाब्धिरमोघवर्षनृपतिः श्रीवीरसिंहासनम् ॥१९॥

i.e., Gōvindarāja IV succeeded Amōghavarsha II, but as he died shortly afterwards on account of excessive sexual habits his feudatories requested Amōghavarsha III, the son of Jagattunga, to take the responsibilities of the government of the Raṭṭas and made him their king.

---

1 In the copper grant dated Shaka S. 855 (A.D. 933) of Sānglī it is thus stated:—

सामर्थ्ये सति निन्दिता प्रवहिता नैवाग्रजे क्रूरता
बन्धुस्त्रीगमनादिभिः कुचरितैरावर्जितं नायशः ।
शौचाशौचपराङ्मुखं न च भिया पैशाच्यमङ्गीकृतं
त्यागेनासमसाहसैश्च भुवने यः साहसाङ्कोऽभवत् ॥

i.e., Gōvindarāja did not wrong his elder brother, nor was he guilty of incest, nor of cruelty, but he had earned the title of 'Sāhasānka' for his courage and self-abnegation.

We presume from this statement that he might have been blamed of such crimes in his lifetime, to refute which he was obliged to make such mention in his copper plate.

2 Journal Bombay Branch Royal Asiatic Society, Vol. XVIII, page 251 and Epigraphia Indica, Vol. V, page 192.

The following were the titles of Amōghavarsha III (Baddiga):—Shrī Pṛithvīvallabha, Mahārājādhirāja, Paramēshvara, Paramabhaṭṭāraka, etc.

He was a wise and powerful ruler, and a devotee of Shiva. He married Kundakadēvī, the daughter of Yuvarāja I (king of Tripuri or Tēnvar),[1] of the Kalachuri (Haihaya) dynasty.

From the inscription[2] of Hēbbāla we understand that the daughter of Baddiga (Amōghavarsha III) was married to king Satyavākya Kōnguṇivarma Pēramāṇaḍi Bhūtuga II, of the western Ganga dynasty to whom a large territory was given in dowry.

Baddiga may have ascended the throne about V.S. 992 (A.D. 935). He had 4 sons:—Kṛishṇarāja, Jagattunga, Khōṭṭiga, and Nirupama. His daughter's name was Rēvakanimmaḍi, and she was the elder sister of Kṛishṇarāja III.

17. KṚISHṆARĀJA III.

He was the eldest son and successor of Baddiga (Amōghavarsha III). Kannara also appears to be the 'Prākṛita' form of his name. His titles have been known to be as follows:—

Akālavarsha, Mahārājādhirāja, Paramēshvara, Paramamāhēshvara, Paramabhaṭṭāraka, Pṛithvivallabha, Shrī Pṛithvīvallabha, Samastabhuvanāshraya, Kandhārapuravarādhīshvara, etc.

From the inscription of Ātkūr we learn that he killed king Rājāditya (Mūvaḍichōla) of the Chōla dynasty in a battle near the place named Takkōla about V.S. 1006-7 (A.D. 949-50),[3] but in fact he was treacherously killed by the Satyavākya Kōnguṇivarma Peramānaḍi Bhūtuga of the western Ganga dynasty,

1 Bhārata-kē-Prāchīna Rājavamsha, Vol. I, page 42.

2 Epigraphia Indica, Vol. IV, page 351.

3 Epigraphia Indica, Vol. II, page 171. The time of the death of Rājāditya is supposed to be V. S. 1006 (A.D. 949).

for which act Kṛishṇarāja gave him the districts of Banavāsī, etc.

In the inscription[1] of Tirukkalukkunram, Kṛishṇa III is stated to have acquired the territories of Kānchī and Tanjōr.

From the inscription of Dēōlī[2] it appears that Kṛishṇa III killed king Dantiga of Kānchī and Vappuga, defeated king Antiga of the Pallava dynasty, protected the Kalachurīs of the Central India against the invasion of the Gurjaras[3] and defeated many other hostile kings. The feudatory chiefs from the Himalayas to Ceylon and from the Eastern sea to the western sea acknowledged his supremacy. He granted a village in charity to commemorate the illustrious services of his younger brother Jagattunga. Kṛishṇa III had acquired considerable power even during his father's lifetime.

In the inscription[4] (of Lakshmēshvara), dated Shaka S. 890 (A.D. 968-9), it is stated that by his order Mārasiṃha II defeated the Gurjara king, while Kṛishṇa III himself was like an incarnation of death for the kings of the Chōla dynasty.

From the inscriptions of Kyāsnoor and Dhārwār we understand that his chief feudatory Kaliviṭṭa, of the Chaillakētana dynasty, was the governor of Banavāsī in V.S. 1002-1003 (A.D. 945-46).[5] In one of the inscriptions[6] of the Raṭṭas of Saundattī it is stated that Kṛishṇa III having appointed Pṛithvīrāma as a chief feudatory had dignified the Raṭṭa family of Saundattī. The

1 Epigraphia Indica, Vol. III, page 234.

2 Indian Antiquary, Vol. V, page 192.

3 These Gurjaras might be the followers of the Chālukya king Mūlarāja of Anhilwāḍā and they attempted to take possession of Kālinjar and Chitrakūṭa.

4 India Antiquary, Vol. VII, page 104.

5 Bombay Gazetteer, Vol. I, Part II, Page 420.

6 Bombay Gazetteer, Vol. I, part II, page 552.

Yādava king Vandiga (Vaddiga) of Sēuṇa (district) was also a feudatory of Kṛishṇa III.

About 16 inscriptions and 2 copper grants of Kṛishṇa's reign have been found, seven of which bear Shaka Samvats while the remaining 8 bear the king's regnal years. The description of these is as follows:—

The first copper grant[1] of Shaka S. 862 (V.S. 997=A.D. 940), found at Dēōlī, speaks of a charitable grant made by Kṛishṇa III in memory of his deceased brother Jagattunga.

An inscription[2] of Shaka S. 867 (V.S. 1002=A.D. 845) found at Sālōṭagī (Bījāpur) contains a mention of a school opened by his minister Nārāyaṇa, where students used to come from various parts of the country.

In the second inscription[3] of Shaka S. 871 (V.S. 1006=A.D. 949), found at Shōlāpur, this king is stated to be a Chakravartī (Emperor). The third inscription[4] of Shaka S. 872 (V.S. 1007=A.D. 950), found at Atkūr (Mysore), shows that king Krishṇa III awarded the district of Banavāsī, etc., to king Bhūtuga II of the western Ganga dynasty for his killing Chōla king Rājāditya. The fourth inscription[5] of Shaka S. 873 (V.S. 1008=A.D. 951) is found at Soratūr (Dhārwār); the fifth of Shaka S. 875 (V.S. 1014=A.D. 957),[6] at Shōlāpur; and the sixth[7] of Shaka S. 976 (V.S. 1011=A.D. 954), at Chinchlī.

The second copper grant[8] of this king, bearing Shaka S. 880 (V.S. 1015=A.D. 958), found at Karhad, indicates that Kṛishṇa III, while invading the South, laid waste

1 Epigraphia Indica, Vol. V, page 192.
2 Do. do. IV, page 60.
3 Do. do. VII, page 194.
4 Do. do. II, page 171.
5 Indian Antiquary, Vol. XII, page 257.
6 Epigraphia Indica, Vol. VII, page 196.
7 Kielhorn's list of the Southern inscriptions of India, No. 97.
8 Epigraphia Indica, Vol. IV, page 281.

the province of Chōla,[1] conquered the territory of Pāṇḍya, subjugated the king of Ceylon, exacted tributes from the'Mānaḍlika' rulers and erected a monumental tower at Rāmēshvaram to commemorate these victories.

He also granted a village for the construction of the temples of Kālapriya, Ganḍamārtaṇḍa and Kṛishṇēshvara.

His seventh inscription,[2] dated Shaka S. 884 (V.S. 1019=A.D. 962), was found at Dēvī Hosūr.

Eight inscriptions in Tamil language bearing no date are of his 16th[3], 17th[4], 19th[5], 21st[6], 22nd[7], 24th[8] and 26th[9] regnal years. There are two inscriptions of the 17th[10] year. The ninth inscription of Lakshmēshvara bears neither the date nor the regnal year. In these also he is described as the conqueror[11] of Kānchī and Tanjaī (Tanjor).

The Vīra Chōla, mentioned in the inscription of the 26th regnal year, might be Gangavāṇa Pṛithvīpati II.

Kṛishṇa III also used to assist his father in the conduct of the Government. He dethroned Rāchamalla I, of the western Ganga dynasty, and installed his own brother-in-law Bhūtuga II,[12] in his place. He defeated Kalachuri (Haihaya) Sahasrārjuna, king of Chēdi, and a relative of his mother and wife. The king of Gujrāt was also afraid of his bravery.

---

1 This fact is also supported by an inscription of Kṛishṇarāja III, found at the village named Jūrā. (Epigraphia Indica, Vol. XIX, page 287). This event probably took place in V. S. 1004 (A. D. 947).)

2 Kielhorn's list of the inscriptions of Southern India, No. 89.

3 South Indian inscriptions, Vol. III, No. 7, page 12.

4 Epigraphia Indica, Vol. VII, page 135.

5 Do. do. III, page 285.

6 Do. do. VII, page 142.

7 Do. do. VII, page 143.

8 Do. do. VII, page 144.

9 Do. do. IV, page 82.

10 Do. do. III, page 284.

11 At that time the Pallavas ruled at Kānchī and the Chōlas at Tanjor.

12 From an inscription in the Tamil language of a later date it appears that Rāchamalla was also killed by Bhūtuga.

As an inscription of his 26th regnal year has been found, it is certain that he ruled at least for 26 years.

The drama named 'Yashastilaka Champū,' written by Sōmadēva, was completed[1] in Shaka S. 881 (V.S. 1016=A.D. 959), in the reign of Kṛishṇa III, and in it Kṛishṇa III has been described as the conqueror of Chēra, Chōla, Pāṇḍya, and Simhala. (A book named 'Nītivākyāmrita'[2] on politics was also written by the same Sōmadēva).

We have come across "Parama Māhēshvara" as one of the titles of the king which shows that he was a devotee of Shiva. He may have ascended the throne about V.S. 996 (A.D. 939).

He was a great king and his kingdom extended even beyond the Ganges.

The famous poet Pōnna of the Canarese language, who followed Jainism and wrote the 'Shānti Purāṇa,' also flourished in his reign. Pleased with his talents Kṛishṇa III decorated him with the title of "Ubhayabhāshā Chakravartī." The poet laureate Pushpadanta also came to Mānyakhēṭa during his time and compiled the Jain 'Mahāpurāṇa' in the 'Apabhramsha' language, under the patronage of his minister Bharata. The book contains a mention of the plunder of Mānyakhēṭa, which took place in V.S. 1029. This shows that the book in question was completed in the time of Khōṭṭiga, the successor of Kṛishṇa III.

This Pushpadanta had also written the books named "Yashōdharacharita" and "Nāgakumāracharita" which contain a mention of Nanna, the son of Bharata. These books too may have been written in the time of the successors of Kṛishṇa III.

---

1 When Sōmadēva compiled this work, he was living in the capital of Prince Baddiga, the eldest son of the Chālukya Arikēsarī, a feudatory of king Krishṇa III.

2 Jain Sāhitya Samshōdhaka, part II, issue 3, page 35.

In the Jain Library of Karanjā there is a book named "Jvālā mālinī Kalpa" at the end of which it is stated[1]:—

अष्टाशतसैकषष्टिप्रमाणशकसंवत्सरेष्वतीतेषु
श्रीमान्यखेटकटके पर्वण्यक्षयतृतीयायाम् ।
शतदलसहितचतुःशतपरिमाणग्रन्थरचनया युक्तम्
श्रीकृष्णराजराज्ये समाप्तमेतन्मतं देव्याः ॥

i.e., this work was finished in Shaka S. 861, in the reign of king Kṛishṇarāja.

This shows that Kṛishṇarāja was ruling in Shaka S. 861 (V.S. 996=A.D. 939).

18. KHŌṬṬIGA.

He was the son of Amōghavarsha III. He succeeded his elder brother Kṛishṇarāja III.

It is stated in the copper grant[2] of Shaka S. 984, found at Karḍā (Khāndēsh):—

स्वर्गमधिरूढे च ज्येष्ठे भ्रातरि श्रीकृष्णराजदेवे-
युवराजदेवदुहितरि कन्दुकदेव्याममोघवर्षनृपा-
ज्जातः खोट्टिगदेवो नृपतिरभूद् भुवनविख्यातः ॥१६॥

i.e., on the death of his elder brother Kṛishṇarāja-dēva, Khōṭṭigadēva,[3] son of Amōghavarsha and Kandakadēvī (the daughter of Yuvarājadēva), ascended the throne.

Though Khōṭṭiga had an elder brother named Jagattunga, yet, as he predeceased Kṛishṇarāja, Khōṭṭiga succeeded him.

The following were the titles of Khōṭṭiga:—Nityavarsha; Raṭṭakandarpa, Mahārājādhirāja, Paramēshvara, Paramabhaṭṭāraka, Shrī Pṛithvīvallabha, etc.

An inscription[4] in the Canarese language of Shaka S.893 (V.S. 1028=A.D. 971), contains a title of this king,

1 Jain Sāhitya Samshōdhaka, part II, issue 3, pages 145-156.

2 Indian Antiquary, Vol. XII, page 264.

3 This seems to be only a 'Prakrita' form of the king's real name, mention of which has not yet been found anywhere.

4 Indian Antiquary, Vol. XII, page 255.

'Nityavarsha' and a mention of his feudatory Pēramānaḍi Mārasimha II, of the western Ganga dynasty. This Mārasimha had under his sway 96,000 villages? of Gangavāḍī, 300 of Bēlavala and 300 of Purigēra.

An inscription[1] of the time of Paramāra king Udayāditya, found at Udaipur (Gwalior), contains the following lines:—

श्रीहर्षदेव इति खोट्टिगदेवलक्ष्मीं
जग्राह यो युधि नगादसमः प्रतापः [१२]

i.e., Shri Harsha (Sīyaka II of the Paramāra dynasty of Mālwā) had seized the kingdom from Khōṭṭigadēva.

At the end of the Prākrita dictionary named 'Pāiyalachchhī Nāmamālā,' written by Dhanapāla, it is stated:—

विक्कमकालस्स गए अउणत्तीसुत्तरे सहस्सम्मि ।
मालवनरिन्दधाडीए लूडिए मन्नखेडम्मि ॥२७६॥

i. e., in Vikrama S. 1029, the king of Mālwā plundered the city of Mānyakhēta.

These show that after defeating Khōṭṭiga, Sīyaka II may have looted his capital town Mānyakhēṭa. Just about the date of this event Dhanapāla had compiled the aforesaid dictionary (Pāiyalachchī Nāmamālā) for his sister Sundarā. In this warfare Kankadēva, king of Vāgaḍa and cousin of king Sīyaka of Mālwā, was killed and king Khōṭṭiga also fell on the field.

This fact is also borne out by the Jain 'Mahāpurāṇa' written by Pushpadanta.

After this event the great power of Rāshṭrakūṭas of the Deccan began to decline.

King Khōṭṭiga may have succeeded to the throne about V.S. 1023 (A.D. 966) and died leaving no male issue.

---

1 Journal Bengal Asiatic Society, Vol. IX, page 549.

19. KARKARĀJA II.

He was the son of Nirupama, the youngest son of Amōghavarsha III. He succeeded his own uncle Khōṭṭigadēva. The other forms of his name were Kakka, Karkara, Kakkara and Kakkala. His titles were Amōghavarsha, Nṛipatunga, Vīranārāyaṇa, Nūtana Pārtha, Ahītamārtaṇḍa, Rājatrinētra, Mahārājādhirāja, Paramēshvara, Paramamāhēshvara, Paramabhaṭṭāraka, Prithvīvallabha, Vallabhanarēndra, etc. From the title 'Parama Māhēshvara' it appears that this king was also a Shaiva.

In a copper grant[1] of Shaka S. 894 (V.S. 1029=A.D. 972), of the reign of Karkarāja, found at Karḍā, the Rāshṭrakūṭas are mentioned as Yādavas.

The capital of his kingdom was Mālkhēḍ and he conquered the territories of the Gurjaras, Chōlas, Huṇas and Pāṇḍyas.

In an inscription[2] of his time of Shaka S. 896 (V.S. 1030=A.D. 973), found at Gunḍūr (Dhārwār) there is a mention of his feudatory Pēramāṇaḍī Mārasimha II of the western Ganga dynasty who had annihilated Nōlambakula of the Pallava dynasty.

Karkarāja II may have ascended the throne in or about V. S. 1029 (A.D. 972).

The weakness of the Rāshṭrakūṭa power resulting from the invasion by Paramāra king Sīyaka II, of Mālwā at the time of Khōṭṭiga, afforded an opportunity to the Chālukyas (Sōlankīs) to regain their lost power. In order to do so, Sōlankī king Tailapa II attacked Karkarāja after V.S. 1030 (A.D. 973) and re-established[3].

1 Indian Antiquary, Vol. XII, page 263,
2 Indian Antiquary, Vol. XII, page 271.
3 In the copper grant of Khārēpāṭan it is stated :—

कक्कलस्तस्य भ्रातृव्यो भुवो भर्ता जनप्रियः ।
आसीत्प्रचण्डधामेव प्रजापार्जितशात्रवः ॥
समरे तं विनिर्जित्य तैलपोऽभून्महीपतिः ।

i.e., the powerful king Karkarāja II. was a nephew of Khōṭṭiga and after defeating him, Tailapa took possession of his kingdom.

the Chālukya (Sōlankī) kingdom of Kalyāṇī. Thus ended the Rāshṭrakūṭa kingdom of the Deccan.[1]

In the inscription[2] of Vijjala of the Kalachuri dynasty, Tailapa is stated to have killed Rāshṭrakūṭa king Karkkara (Karkarāja II) and Raṇakambha (Raṇastambha) who was, perhaps, a relative of king Karkarāja.

The said Sōlankī king Tailapa II had married Jākabbā,[3] the daughter of Rāshṭrakūṭa Bhammaha.

The fact about the destruction of the Rāshṭrakūṭa kingdom of the Deccan by Tailapa II in the time of Karkarāja is further corroborated by the copper plates of Shaka S. 919[4] and 930[5], of kings Aparājita and Raṭṭarāja of the Shilāra dynasty respectively. This Aparājita was a feudatory of the Rāshṭrakūṭas and became independent on their downfall. In the "Vikramānkadēvacharita" (Sarga I, stanza 69) it is stated:—

विश्वम्भराकंटकराष्ट्रकूटसमूलनिर्मूलनकोविदस्य ।
सुखेन यस्यान्तिकमाजगाम चालुक्यचन्द्रस्य नरेंद्रलक्ष्मीः ।

i.e., the state passed on to the Sōlankī king Tailapa II, the destroyer of the Rāshṭrakūṭa kingdom.

An inscription[6] of Shaka S. 904 (V.S. 1039=A.D. 982), found at Shravaṇa Bēlgōla, contains a mention of Indrarāja IV, who was a grandson of Rāshṭrakūṭa king Krishṇarāja III. The mother of this Indra IV was the daughter of Gāngēyadēva of the Ganga dynasty and Indrarāja married the daughter of Rājachūḍāmaṇi.

The titles of this Indrarāja were as follows:—

Raṭṭakandarpadēva, Rājamārtaṇḍa, Chaladanka kāraṇa, Chaladaggalē, Kīrtinārāyaṇa, etc. He is spoken of as a brave and tried warrior and a controller of passions. Having broken the 'Chakravyūha' single-handed, he defeated 18 enemies. Girigē, the wife of Kallara, tried all means to captivate his heart, but he resolutely rejected her overtures. She at last challenged him to battle in which too she was defeated.

---

1 Indian Antiquary, Vol. VIII, page 15.
2 Epigraphia Indica, Vol. V, page 15.
3 Indian Antiquary, Vol. XVI, page 21.
4 Epigraphia Indica, Vol. III, page 272.
5 Do. do. Vol. III, p. 297.
6 Inscriptions at Shravaṇabēlgōla, No. 57, (page 53) A. 17.

After the death of Karkarāja, Pēramānaḍi Mārasimha of the western Ganga dynasty in his efforts to maintain the Rāshṭrakūṭa kingdom, tried his best to obtain the throne for Indra IV. (It has been noted above that Pēramānaḍi Bhūtuga, the father of this Mārasimha, was a brother-in-law of the Rāshṭrakūṭa king Krishṇa III.) This effort was probably made about V.S. 1030 (A.D. 973) but nothing has been known as to its result. This Indra IV courted death by observing total abstinence from food and drink,[1] which is a principle of the Jain theology, and died on the 8th day of the dark half of Chaitra, Shaka S. 904=V. S. 1039 (20th March 982 A.D.).

THE GENEALOGICAL TABLE OF THE RĀSHṬRAKŪṬAS OF MĀNYAKHĒṬA (Deccan.)

1 Dantivarman I.
2 Indrarāja I.
3 Gōvindarāja I.
4 Karkarāja I.

(sons of Karkarāja I:)
5. Indrarāja II.
6. Dantidurga or Dantivarman II.
7. Kṛishṇarāja I.
Nanna.

(sons of Kṛishṇarāja I:)
8. Gōvindarāja II.
9. Dhruvarāja.

(sons of Dhruvarāja:)
10. Gōvindarāja III. (Jagattunga I),
11. Amōghavarsha I.
12. Kṛishṇarāja II.
Indrarāja (originator of the 2nd branch of Gujrat).
Shauchakamba (Kambayya, Stambha or Raṇāvalōka).

(sons of Kṛishṇarāja II:)
Jagattunga II.
Dantivarman.

(sons of Jagattunga II:)
13. Indrarāja III.
16. Amōghavarsha III (Baddiga).

(sons of Indrarāja III:)
14. Amōghavarsha II.
15. Gōvindarāja IV.

(children of Amōghavarsha III:)
17. Kṛishṇarāja III.
Jagattunga III.
18. Khōṭṭiga.
Nirupama.
A daughter named Rēvakanimmaḍi.

(son of Kṛishṇarāja III:) Indrarāja. IV.
(son of Nirupama:) 19. Karkarāja II.

1 Epigraphia Indica, Vol. IV, page 182.

STATEMENT GIVING PARTICULARS OF THE RĀSHṬRAKŪṬAS OF MĀNYAKHĒṬA (DECCAN).

Name.	Relation.	Special Titles.	Known Periods.	Contemporary Kings.
1. Dantivarman I ..				
2. Indrarāja I	Son of No. 1.			
3. Gōvindarāja I ..	Do. No. 2.			
4. Karkarāja I	Do. No. 3.			
5. Indrarāja II	Do. No. 4.			
6. Dantidurga (Dantivarman II) ..	Do. No. 5.	Mahārājādhirāja.	Sh. S. 675.	Western Chālukya Kīrtivarman.
7. Kṛishṇarāja I ..	Brother of No. 5.		Sh. S. 690, (692) 694.	Rāhappa and Kīrtivarman.
8. Gōvindarāja II ..	Son of No. 7.	Do.	Sh. S. 692, (697, 701 705.)	
9 Dhruvarāja	Brother of No. 8.	Do.	Sh. S. 697, 701, (715).	Pratihāra Vatsarāja.
10. Gōvindarāja III ..	Son of No. 9.	Do.	Sh. S 716, 726, 730, 734, 735.	Mārāsharva, Dantiga of Kānchī, Indrāyudha, Vatsarāja (or Varaha) and Vijayāditya.
11. Amōghavarsha I ..	Do. No. 10.	Do.	Sh. S. 738, 749, (757) 765, 775, (773) 782, 787, 788, 789, (799).	Kapardī II of the Shilāra dynasty, Pṛithvīpati, Karkarāja, Sankarganda and Pullashakti.
12. Kṛishṇarāja II ..	Do. No. 11.	Do.	Sh. S. (797) 810 822, (824) 824, 831, (833), 832.	Kalachuri Kōkalla and Shankuka.
13. Indrarāja III ..	Do. No. 12.	Do.	Sh. S. 836, 853.	Kalachuri Ammaṇadēva and Pratihāra Mahīpāla.
14. Amōghavarsha II ..	Do. No 13.			
15. Gōvindarāja IV ..	Brother of No. 14.	Do.	Sh. S. 840, 851, 852, 855.	
16. Baddiga (Amōghavarsha III) ..	Do No. 13.	Do.		Kalachuri Yuvarāja I, and W. Ganga Pēremānaḍi Bhūtuga II.
17. Kṛishṇarāja III ..	Son of No. 16.	Do. Chakravartī.	Sh. S. 861, 862, 867, 871, 872, 873, 875, 876, 880, 881, 884.	Dantiga, Vappuga, Rāchamalla I, Bhūtuga II of W. Ganga dynasty, Aṇṇiga, Rājāditya of Chōla dynasty, Sahasrārjuna of Kalachuri dynasty, Antiga and Pṛithvīrāma.
18. Khōṭṭiga	Brother of No 17.	Mahārājādhirāja.	Sh. S. 893, (V.S. 1029).	Mārasimha and Paramāra Sīyaka II.
19. Karkarāja II ..	Nephew of No. 18.	Do.	Sh. S. 894, 896.	Tailapa II and Mārasimha II.
20. Indrarāja IV ..	Grandson of No. 17.		Sh S. 904.	

By adding 135 to any Shaka Samvat we arrive at the corresponding Vikrama Samvat and by adding 78 we get the corresponding Christian era.

THE RĀSHṬRAKŪṬAS OF LĀTA (GUJRĀT).

FROM BEFORE V. S. 814 (A.D. 757) TO AFTER V.S. 945 (A.D. 888).

First Branch.

It has already been stated that king Dantidurga (Dantivarman II) had seized the kingdom of Chālukya (Sōlankī) king Kīrtivarman II. At the same time the province of Lāta (Southern and Central Gujrāt) had also passed into the possession of the Rāshṭrakūṭas.

A copper grant[1] of Shaka S. 679 (V. S. 814=A.D. 757), of Mahārājādhirāja Karkarāja II of Gujrāt, has been found at Sūrat, which shows that at the time of his victory over the Sōlankīs, king Dantidurga (Dantivarman II) had made this Karkarāja, who was a relative of the former, the king of the province of Lāta (Gujrāt).

From the similarity in the names of the Rāshṭrakūṭa kings of the Deccan and of Gujrāt, it appears that the Rāshṭrakūṭa family of Lāta was a branch of the Rashṭrakūṭa family of the Deccan. In the said copper grant their genealogy is given thus:—

1. Karkarāja I - the first name of this branch known uptill now.
2. Dhruvarāja— son of Karkarāja I.
3. Gōvindarāja—son of Dhruvarāja, married the daughter of Nāgavarman.
4. Karkarāja II—son of Gōvindarāja.

1. Journal Bombay Asiatic Society, Vol. XVI, page 106.

The aforesaid copper grant of Shaka S. 679 (V.S. 814=A.D. 757) is of the time of Karkarāja II. He was a contemporary of the Rāshṭrakūṭa king Dantidurga (Dantivarman II) who had invested him with the ruling powers of Lāta. The following are the titles of king Karkarāja II:—

Parama Māhēshvara, Parama Bhaṭṭāraka, Parmēshvara, Mahārājādhirāja.

This king was a very powerful monarch and a devotee of the God Shiva. Some scholars identify him with Rāhappa who was defeated by the Rāshṭrakūṭa king Krishṇarāja I of the Deccan. It is probable, therefore, that this dynasty came to an end in consequence of this battle. As no inscription, etc., of this family, beyond the one noted above, has been found, there is therefore no further trace of the history of this branch of the Rāshṭrakūṭa rulers.

Second Branch.

In the history of the Rāshṭrakūṭas of the Deccan it has been stated that king Gōvindarāja III had made a grant of the province of Lāta to his younger brother Indrarāja. From the inscriptions of the descendants of this Indrarāja we arrive at the following history of this branch:—

1. INDRARĀJA.

He was the son of king Dhruvarāja and younger brother of Gōvindarāja III of the Rāshṭrakūṭa dynasty of the Deccan, who had made him the ruler of Lāta (Southern and Central Gujrāt).

In the copper grant[1] of Shaka S. 730 (V.S. 865=A.D. 808), of king Gōvinda III, there is a mention of the conquest of Gujrāt, which shows that sometime about this date, Indrarāja got possession of Lāta. This Indra had two sons:—Karkarāja and Gōvindarāja.

1 Epigraphia Indica, Vol. VI, page 242.

2. KARKARĀJA (KAKKARĀJA).

He was the son and successor of Indrarāja. Two copper grants of his time are found. The first[1] is of Shaka S. 734 (V.S. 869=A.D. 812), which shows that Gōvindarāja III of the Rāshṭrakūṭa dynasty of the Deccan made his younger brother Indrarāja, father of Karkarāja, the king of Lāta. The titles of king Karkarāja, *viz.*, Mahā Sāmantādhipati, Lātēshvara and Suvarṇavarsha, are also mentioned in this plate. This king had protected the king of Mālava from the invasion of the king of Gujrāt, who had conquered the Gauḍa and the Banga provinces. The executor of the grant mentioned in this plate is named therein as prince Dantivarman.

The other copper plate[2] is of Shaka S. 738 (V.S. 873= A.D. 817).

In the copper grant[3] of Shaka S. 757 (V.S.892=A.D. 835), of the chief feudatory Dhruvarāja I of Gujrāt, it is stated that having put down the rebellous Rāshṭrakūṭas, king Karkarāja had installed king Amōghavarsha I, of Mānyakhēṭa on the throne of his father (about V.S. 872=A.D. 815).

From this it appears that at the time of the death of Gōvindarāja III, his son, Amōghavarsha I, was a minor, which afforded an opportunity to the feudatory Rāshṭrakūṭas and the Sōlankīs to attempt at dispossessing him of the kingdom but Karkarāja frustrated their attempts.

Karkarāja had a son named Dhruvarāja.

3. GŌVINDARĀJA.

He was the son of Indrarāja and younger brother of Karkarāja. We have found two copper grants of

1 Indian Antiquary, Vol. XII, page 156.

2 Journal Bombay Asiatic Society, Vol. XX, page 135.

3 Indian Antiquary, Vol. XIV, page 199.

his time. The first[1] is of Shaka S. 735 (V.S. 870=A.D. 813) and the second[2] of Shaka S. 749 (V.S. 884=A.D. 827). The first plate speaks of the king's chief feudatory, Buddhavarsha of the Shalukika clan, and contains Gōvindarāja's titles, *viz*, Mahāsāmantādhipati and Prabhūtavarsha. From the other plate, we gather that when Gōvindarāja was at Broach he granted a village for the upkeep of a temple of the Sun god named Jayāditya.

As there exist copper grants of Shaka S. 734 and 738 of Karkarāja, and those of Shaka S. 735 and 749 of his younger brother Gōvindarāja, we understand that the two brothers weilded authority simultaneously for some time.

4. DHRUVARĀJA I.

He was the son of Karkarāja and succeeded to the throne after his uncle Gōvindarāja. The copper grant[3] of Shaka S. 757 (V.S. 892=A.D. 835), mentioned above in the history of Karkarāja, belongs to this king, and contains his titles; *viz*, Mahāsāmantādhipati, Dhārāvarsha and Nirupama.

He had headed a rising against Amōghavarsha I, which obliged the latter to march against him. Dhruvarāja was probably killed in this action, as is evident from the copper grant of Shaka S. 789 (V.S. 924=A.D. 867) found at Begumra.

5. AKĀLAVARSHA.

He was the son and successor of Dhruvarāja. His titles are found to be Shubhatunga and Subhaṭātunga. During his reign, too, relations with the Rāshṭrakūṭas

1 Epigraphia Indica, Vol. III, page 54.
2 Indian Antiquary, Vol. V, page 145.
3 Indian Antiquary, Vol. XIV, page 199.

of the Deccan do not appear to have been friendly.[1] He had three sons:—Dhruvarāja, Dantivarman, and Gōvindarāja.

6. DHRUVARĀJA II.

He was the son and successor of Akālavarsha. In a copper grant[2] of Shaka S. 789 (V.S. 924=A.D. 867) of this king, the executor of the order of charity concerned is named Gōvindarāja. This Gōvindarāja was the son of Shubhatunga (Akālavarsha) and younger brother of Dhruvarāja II. He (Dhruvarāja) had defeated the combined invading armies of Gurjararāja,[3] Vallabha, and Mihira. This Mihira probably was Pratihāra Bhōjadēva of Kanauj, whose title was "Mihira." Mention of a battle with Vallabha shows that this king may have tried to throw off the yoke of suzerainty of the Rāshṭrakūṭa king of Mānyakhēta.[4]

This king had granted in charity the district of Trēnnā to a Brahmaṇa named Ḍhōḍḍhi who maintained with its revenue, a free boarding house where thousands of Brahmaṇas daily received their food, alike in years of scarcity and plenty. His (Dhruvarāja's) younger brother Gōvinda also fought on his side.

7. DANTIVARMAN.

He was the son of Akālavarsha and younger brother of Dhruvarāja II, whom he succeeded. A copper grant[5] of Shaka S. 789 (V.S. 924=A.D. 867) of his time has been found. It contains his titles, *viz.*, Mahāsāmantādhipati, Aparimitavarsha, etc. The charity it speaks of was granted for a Buddhist monastery.

---

1 In the copper grant of Shaka S. 789 of Begumra, it is stated that though his faithless followers foresook him, Akālavarsha regained his paternal kingdom from the army of Vallabha (Amōghavarsha I). Indian Antiquary, Vol. XII, page 181).

2 Indian Antiquary, Vol. XII, page 181.

3 Chāora Kshēmarāja might be the king of Gujrāt at this time.

4 The aforesaid copper grant of Shaka S. 789 further goes to show that when enemies invaded his country all his relatives and even his younger brother deserted him.

5 Epigraphia Indica, Vol. VI, page 287.

From the copper grant of Dhruvarāja, II it appears that the two brothers were not on good terms, but in the plate of Dantivarman I, the latter is described as a devotee of his elder brother Dhruvarāja. Probably, therefore, it might be some other brother referred to in the above plate of Dhruvarāja.

8. KṚISHṆARĀJA.

He was the son and successor of Dantivarman. A copper grant[1] of Shaka S. 810 (V.S. 945=A.D. 888) of his time has been found which appears to be incorrect. His titles are found to be Mahāsāmantādhipati, Akālavarsha, etc.

This Kṛishṇarāja defeated his enemies at Ujjain in the presence of Vallabharāja.

The history of this family is not traceable any further. By thinking over the contents of the copper grant of Shaka S. 832 (V.S. 967=A.D. 910), of Rāshṭrakūṭa Kṛishṇa II of Mānyakhēṭa, we conclude that sometime between Shaka S. 810 (V.S. 945=A.D. 888) and Shaka S. 832 (V.S. 967=A.D. 910) he (Kṛishṇarāja II), having annexed the kingdom of Lāṭa, put an end to the Rāshṭrakūṭa dynasty of Gujrāt.

GENEALOGY OF THE RĀSHṬRAKŪṬAS OF LAṬA (Gujrāt).

(First Branch.)

1. Karkarāja I.
 |
2. Dhruvarāja.
 |
3. Gōvindarāja.
 |
4. Karkarāja II.

(Second Branch.)

Dhruvarāja of Mānyakhēṭa.
 |
1. Indrarāja.
 |
 ├── 2. Karkarāja.
 │ |
 │ 4. Dhruvarāja I.
 │ |
 │ 5. Akālavarsha.
 │ |
 │ ├── 6. Dhruvarāja II.
 │ ├── 7. Dantivarman.
 │ │ |
 │ │ 8. Kṛishṇarāja.
 │ └── Gōvindarāja II.
 └── 3. Gōvindarāja I.

---

1 Indian Antiquary, Vol. XIII, page 66.

STATEMENT GIVING PARTICULARS OF THE RĀSHṬRAHKŪṬAS OF LĀTA (GUJRĀT).

NAME.	SPECIAL TITLE.	RELATION.	ASCERTAINED DATES.	CONTEMPORARIES.
			(First Branch.)	
1. Karkarāja I.. ..				
2. Dhruvarāja		Son of No. 1.		
3. Gōvindarāja ...		„ 2.		Nāgavarman.
4. Karkarāja II ..	Mahārājādhirāja.	„ 3.	Shaka S. 679.	Rāshṭrakūṭa Dantidurga (Dantivarman II) and Kṛishṇarāja I.
			(Second Branch.)	
1. Indrarāja		Younger brother of Gōvinda III of Mānyakhēṭa.		Rāshṭrakūṭa Gōvindarāja III.
2. Karkarāja	Mahāsāmantādhipati.	Son of No. 1.	Shaka S. 734 & 738.	Amōghavarsha I.
3. Gōvindarāja ..	Do.	Brother of No. 2.	„ 735 & 749.	Amōghavarsha I.
4. Dhruvarāja I ..	Do.	Son of No. 2.	„ 757.	Amōghavarsha I.
5. Akālavarsha ...	Do.	„ 4.		Amōghavarsha I.
6. Dhruvarāja II ..	Do.	„ 5.	„ 789.	Mihira (Pratihāra Bhōja).
7. Dantivarman ..	Do.	Brother of No. 6.	„ 789.	
8. Kṛishṇarāja.. ..	Do.	Son of No. 7.	„ 810.	Rāshṭrakūṭa Krishṇarāja II.

THE RAṬṬAS (RĀSHṬRAKŪṬAS) OF SAUNDATTI.

FROM ABOUT V. S. 932 (A.D. 875) TO ABOUT V.S. 1287 (A.D. 1230).

It has already been stated that Chālukya (Sōlankī) Tailapa II had seized the kingdom of Mānyakhēṭa (Deccan) from the Rāshṭrakūṭa king Karkarāja II. It can be inferred from the inscriptions of these two kings that this event, perhaps, took place just after V.S. 1030 (A.D. 973). But from other inscriptions we learn that long after the downfall of the Rāshṭrakūta kingdom petty principalities of its younger off-shoots outlived and that they became feudatories of the Chālukyas (Sōlankīs).

We are able to trace two such branches of the Rāshṭrakūṭas that existed in the modern Dhārwār district of the Bombay Presidency and flourished one after the other at Saundatti (Kuntal in the Belgaum district). Often they are mentioned as Raṭṭas in their inscriptions.

(The First Branch)

1. MĒRAḌA.

This is the first name traceable of this branch.

2. PṚITHVĪRĀMA.

He was the son and successor of Mērаḍa. An inscription[1] of Shaka S. 797 (V.S. 932=A.D. 875) of this chief has been found, in which he is mentioned as belonging to the Raṭṭa race.

1 Journal Bombay Asiatic Society, Vol. X, page 194.

He was a feudatory of the Rāshṭrakūṭa king Kṛishṇarāja and ruler of Saundatti. From the date of this inscription we infer that he was a contemporary of Rāshṭrakūṭa king Kṛishṇarāja II, but we have found another inscription of Pṛithvīrama's grandson Shāntivarman of the Shaka S. 902 (V.S. 1037=A.D. 980). As there is an interval of 105 years between the dates of these two inscriptions, which seems somewhat extraordinary, it is probable, therefore, that Pṛithvīrāma's inscription was prepared afterwards and that this is the cause of the inaccuracy in the date. Again, he might be a contemporary not of the Rāshṭrakūṭa king Kṛishṇarāja II. but of Kṛishṇarāja III. This Pṛithvīrāma followed Jainism and was created a chief feudatory (Mahāsāmtādhipati) about V.S. 997 (A.D. 940).

3. PIṬṬUGA.

He was the son and successor of Pṛithvīrāma. He defeated Ajavarman in battle. His wife's name was Nījikabbē.

4. SHĀNTIVARMAN.

He was the son of Piṭṭuga and succeeded to the throne after him. An inscription[1] of Shaka S. 902 (V.S. 1037=A.D. 980) of this king has been found, in which he has been described as a feudatory of the western Chālukya (Sōlankī) king Tailapa II. His wife's name was Chanḍikabbē. After this we are unable to trace the history of this branch.

(*The Second Branch.*)

1. NANNA.

This is the first name traced of the second branch of the Raṭṭa rulers of Saundatti.

---

1 Journal Bombay Asiatic Society, Vol. X, page 204.

2. KĀRTAVĪRYA I.

He was the son and successor of Nanna. An inscription[1] of Shaka S. 902 (V.S. 1037=A.D. 980) of this king has been found. He was a feudatory of the Sōlankī king Tailapa II and governor of Kūṇḍi in Dhārwār of which district he had fixed the boundaries. It is probable that this chief may have put an end to the first branch of Saundatti, having wrested authority from Shāntivarman. He had two sons:—Dāyima and Kanna.

3. DĀYIMA (DĀVARI).

He was the son and successor of Kārtavīrya I.

4. KANNA (KANNAKAIRA I).

He was the son of Kārtavīrya and younger brother of Dāyima whom he succeeded. He had two sons, Ērēga and Anka.

5. ĒRĒGA (ĒRĒYAMMARASA).

He was the son and successor of Kanna I. An inscription[2] of his time, of Shaka S. 962 (V.S. 1097=A.D. 1040), has been found in which he is described as the chief feudatory of the Chālukya (Sōlankī) king Jayasimha II (Jagadēkamalla), the ruler of Laṭṭalūra, and was decorated with the five high titles. He was an expert musician. He was also called Raṭṭa Nārāyaṇa. As there was a golden image of Garuḍa on his flag he was further called "Singana Garuḍa". An ensign conveyed on an elephant, with a band called "Ṭivili" (like the one played in the processions of the Rāshṭrakūṭas of the Deccan) used to decorate his procession.

The name of his son was Sēna (Kālasēna).

---

1 Kielhorn's list of South Indian Inscriptions, page 26, No. 141.

2 Indian Antiquary, Vol. XIX, page 164.

6. ANKA.

He was the son of Kanna I and succeeded his elder brother Ērēga. An inscription[1] of his time, of Shaka S. 970 (V.S. 1105=A.D. 1048), has been found in which he is mentioned as a chief feudatory of the western Chālukya (Sōlankī) Trailōkyamalla (Sōmēshvara I). Perhaps, another broken inscription of his time has also been found which, too, is of the same year.

7. SĒNA (KĀLASĒNA I).

He was the son of Ērēga and a successor of his uncle Anka. He married Mailaladēvī from whom he had two sons:—Kanna and Kārtavīrya.

8. KANNA (KANNAKAIRA II).

He was the son and successor of Sēna (Kālasēna I). One copper grant and one inscription of his time have been found. The copper grant[2] is of Shaka S. 1004 (V.S. 1139=A.D. 1082) in which this Kanna II of the Raṭṭa race is mentioned as a chief feudatory of the Sōlankī (western Chālukya) king Vikramāditya VI. It also appears from this plate that Kanna had purchased many villages from Mahāmaṇḍalēshvara Munja, king of Bhōgavatī (grandson of Bhīma and son of Sindarāja), who belonged to the Sinda dynasty which is stated as the gem of the Nāga race.

The inscription[3] mentioned above is of Shaka S. 1009 (V.S. 1144=A.D. 1087). In it he is mentioned as Mahāmaṇḍalēshvara (the chief feudatory).

9. KĀRTAVĪRYA II.

He was the son of Sēna I and younger brother of Kanna II. He was also called Kaṭṭa. His wife's name was Bhāgaladēvī or Bhāglāmbikā. Three inscriptions

1 Journal Bombay Asiatic Society, Vol. X, page 172.
2 Epigraphia Indica, Vol. III, page 308.
3 Journal Bombay Asiatic Society, Vol. X, page 287.

of his time have been found. The first[1], found from Saundatti, shows that he was a chief feudatory of the western Chālukya (Sōlankī) king Sōmēshvara II and ruler of Laṭṭalūra. The second[2] inscription is of Shaka S. 1009 (V.S. 1144=A.D. 1087); in it he is mentioned as the chief feudatory of Vikramāditya VI, the successor of Sōmēshvara.

The third inscription[3] is of Shaka S. 1045 (V.S. 1180=A.D. 1123). But his son Sēna II had assumed power before this date.

By looking into the inscriptions of Kanna II and Kārtavīrya II, we understand that the two brothers had ruled together.

10. SĒNA (KĀLASĒNA II).

He was the son and successor of Kārtavīrya II. An inscription[4] of his time, of Shaka S. 1018 (V.S. 1153=A.D. 1096), has been found. He was a contemporary of Chālukya (Sōlankī) Vikramāditya VI, and his son Jayakarṇa. Jayakarṇa's period has been ascertained to be from V.S. 1159 (A.D. 1102) to V.S. 1178 (A.D. 1121). So Sēna II may have lived sometime between these dates. The name of his wife was Lakshmīdēvī.

As we have found an inscription of his father, of the year Shaka S. 1045 (V.S. 1180=A.D. 1123), it appears that the father and the son both had wielded the authority together.

11. KĀRTAVĪRYA (KAṬṬAMA III).

He was the son and successor of Sēna (Kālasēna II). His wife's name was Padmaladēvī.

A broken inscription[5] of his time has been found at Kōṇṇūr in which his titles are mentioned as Mahāman-

1 Journal Bombay Asiatic Society, Vol. X, page 213.
2 Do. do. do. do. 173.
3 Indian Antiquary, Vol. XIV, page 15.
4 Journal Bombay Asiatic Society, Vol. X, page 194.
5 Archaeological Survey of India, Vol. III, page 103.

ḍalēshvara and Chakravartī, which shows that in the beginning he remained a feudatory of the western Chālukya (Sōlankī) kings Jagadēkamalla II and Tailapa III. But sometime after V.S. 1222 (A.D. 1165), due to the decline of the power of the Sōlankī and the Kalachurī (Haihaya) dynasties, he became independent and may have assumed the title of Chakravartī.

From an inscription of Shaka S. 1109 (past) (V.S. 1244=A.D. 1187) it appears that at that time one Bhāyidēva ruled over Kūnḍi, who was an administrator of criminal justice under Sōlankī Sōmēshvara IV. From this we infer that the Raṭṭas might not have attained full success in gaining independence upto that time.

The name of Kārtavīrya is also mentioned in the inscriptions,[1] found at Khānpur (Kōlhāpur State), of Shaka S. 1066 (V.S. 1200=A.D. 1143) and Shaka S. 1084 (past) (V.S. 1219=A.D. 1162) and also in the inscription[2] of the Bēlgāum district of Shaka S. 1086 (V.S. 1221=A.D. 1164).

12. LAKSHMĪDĒVA I.

He was the son and successor of Kārtavīrya III. His other names Lakshmaṇa and Lakshmīdhara are also found. His wife's name was Chandrikādēvī (or Chandaladēvī).

An inscription[3] of Shaka S. 1130 (V.S. 1265=A.D. 1209) has been found at Haṇṇikēri, which appears to be of his time. As inscriptions have been found of his sons Kārtavīrya IV and Mallikārjuna from Shaka S. 1121 to 1141 and 1127 to 1131 respectively, it appears ordinarily impossible that he lived in Shaka S. 1130. But, if we suppose that the period of the

1 Carn.-dēsa inscriptions, Vol. II, pages 547-548.
2 Indian Antiquary, Vol. IV, page 116.
3 Bombay Gazetteer, Vol. I, part II, page 556.

reigns of the father and sons had run concurrently, as we have done in cases of Kanna II and Kārtavīrya II, then the enigma disappears. But, so long as convincing proofs of the above fact are not forthcoming, nothing can be said with certainty.

He had two sons:—Kārtavīrya and Mallikārjuna.

13. KARTAVĪRYA IV.

He was the eldest son of Lakshmīdēva I. Six inscriptions and one copper grant of his time have been found. The first inscription[1] of Shaka S. 1121 (past) (V.S. 1257=A.D. 1200) is found at Sankēshvara (Bēlgāum district). The second inscription[2] is of Shaka S. 1124 (V.S. 1258=A.D. 1201). The third[3] and fourth[4] inscriptions are of Shaka S. 1126 (past) (V.S. 1261=A.D. 1204). The fifth[5] is of Shaka S. 1127 (V.S. 1261=A.D. 1204). In this inscription Kārtavīrya IV has been mentioned as the ruler of Laṭanūr and his capital is named Vēṇugrāma. His younger brother Yuvarāja Mallikārjuna is also mentioned in it. The copper grant[6] of his time is of Shaka S. 1131 (V.S. 1265=A.D. 1208), which also contains a mention of his younger brother and heir—apparent, Mallikārjuna.

The sixth inscription[7] is of Shaka S. 1141 (V.S. 1275= A.D. 1218). This king bore the title of Mahāmaṇḍalēshvara. He had two queens, Ēchaladēvī and Mādēvī.

14. LAKSHMĪDĒVA II.

He was the son and successor of Kārtavīrya IV. An

1 Carn.-dēsa inscriptions, Vol. II, page 561.
2 Graham's Kolhapur, page 415, No. 9.
3 Carn.-dēsa inscriptions, Vol. II, page 571.
4 Carn.-dēsa inscriptions, Vol. II, page 576.
5 Journal Bombay Asiatic Society, Vol. X, page 220.
6 Indian Antiquary Vol. XIX, p. 245.
7 Journal Bombay Asiatic Society, Vol. X, page 240.

inscription[1] of his time of Shaka S. 1151 (V.S. 1285=A.D. 1228) has been found in which his title is mentioned as Mahāmaṇḍalēshvara. His mother's name was Mādēvī.

As no record of this family bearing a date later than Shaka S. 1151 has yet been found, it appears that this branch of the Raṭṭas, probably, ceased to exist at this stage and their kingdom was seized by the Yādava king Singhaṇa of Deogiri. This event may have occurred about V.S. 1287 (A.D. 1230). But the districts north, south and east of Kūṇḍi had already passed out of the possession of Lakshmīdēva II even before this date.

In the copper plate[2] of Shaka S. 1160 (V.S. 1295=A.D. 1238) of Haralahalli, Vīchaṇa, a feudatory of Yādava king Singhaṇa of Deogiri, is stated to have defeated the Raṭṭas.

A copper plate[3] has been found from Sītābaldī of Shaka S. 1008 (1009) (V.S. 1144=A.D. 1087) of Rāṇaka Dhāḍibhaṇḍaka (Dhāḍidēva), the chief feudatory of the western Chālukya (Sōlankī) Vikramāditya VI (Tribhuvanamalla), in which this Dhāḍibhaṇḍaka is stated to be of the Mahā Rāshṭrakūṭa race and to have come from Laṭalūr.

In the inscription[4] of Shaka S. 1052 (V.S. 1186=A.D. 1129) found at Khānpur (Kōlhāpur State) there is a mention of Raṭṭa Ankidēva, a chief feudatory of Sōlankī Sōmēshvara III. But there is no trace as to how he was connected with the above-mentioned branches of the Raṭṭas.

---

1 Journal Bombay Asiatic Society, Vol. X, page 260.

2 Journal Bombay Asiatic Society, Vol. X, page 260; and Chronology of India, page 182.

3 Epigraphia Indica, Vol. III, page 305.

4 Epigraphia Indica, Vol. III, page 305.

In the inscription[1] found at Bahuriband (Jabbalpur), there is a mention of the Rāshṭrakūṭa Gōlhaṇadēva, who was a chief feudatory of king Gayakarṇa of the Kalachurī (Haihaya) dynasty. This inscription is of the 12th century, but it gives no clue as to the branch of the Rāshṭrakūṭas to which this Gōlhaṇadēva belonged.

THE GENEALOGY OF THE RAṬṬAS OF SAUNDATTI.

(*First Branch.*)

1. Mēraḍa.
2. Pṛithvīrāma.
3. Piṭṭuga.
4. Shāntivarman.

(*Second Branch.*)

1. Nanna.
2. Kārtavīrya I.
   - 3. Dāyima.
   - 4. Kanna I.
     - 5. Ērēga.
       - 7. Sēna I.
         - 8. Kanna II.
         - 9. Kārtavīrya II.
           - 10. Sēna II.
           - 11. Kārtavīrya III.
           - 12. Lakshmīdēva I.
             - 13. Kārtavīrya IV.
               - 14. Lakshmīdēva II.
             - Mallikārjuna.
     - 6. Anka.

---

1 Archaeological Survey of India, Vol. IX, page 40.

STATEMENT GIVING PARTICULARS OF THE RAṬṬAS OF SAUNDATTI (SUGANDHAVARTĪ).

No.	Name.	Special Title.	Relation.	Ascertained Dates.	Contemporaries.
			(First	Branch.)	
1	Mēraḍa				
2	Pṛithvīrāma.. ..		Son of No. 1.	Shaka S. 797.	Rāshṭrakūṭa king Kṛishṇa.
3	Piṭṭuga		Do. 2.		Arjunavarman.
4	Shāntivarman ..		Do. 3.	Shaka S. 902.	Sōlankī Tailapa II and Raṭṭa Kārtavīrya I.
			(Second	Branch.)	
1	Nanna..				
2	Kārtavīrya I ..		Son of No. 1.	Shaka S. 902.	Sōlankī Tailapa II and Raṭṭa Shāntivarman.
3	Dāyima		Do. 2.		
4	Kanna I		Brother of No. 3.		
5	Ērēga..	Mahāsāmanta.	Son of No. 4.	Shaka S. 962.	Sōlankī Jayasimha II (Jagadēkamalla).
6	Anka	Do.	Brother of No. 5.	Shaka S. 970.	Sōlankī Sōmēshvara I (Trailōkyamalla).
7	Sēna I..		Son of No. 5.		
8	Kanna II	Do.	Do. 7.	Shaka S. 1004 & 1009.	Sōlankī Sōmēshvara II, Vikramāditya VI and Munja of the Sinda clan.
9	Kārtavīrya II ..	Mahāmaṇḍalēshvara.	Brother of No. 8.	Shaka S. 1009 & 1045.	Sōlankī Sōmēshvara II, and Vikramāditya VI.
10	Sēna II	Do.	Son of No. 9.	Shaka S. 1018.	Sōlankī Vikramāditya VI and Jayakarṇa.
11	Kārtavīrya III ..	Mahāmaṇḍalēshvara and Chakravartī.	Do. 10.	Shaka S. 1066, 1084, (past) and 1086.	Sōlankī Jagadēkamalla II and Tailapa III.
12	Lakshmīdēva I ..		Do. 11.	Shaka S. 1130.	
13	Kārtavīrya IV ..	Mahāmaṇḍalēshvara.	Do. 12.	Shaka S. 1121 (past) 1124, 1126 (past), 1127, 1131 & 1141.	
	Mallikārjuna ..	Yuvarāja.	Brother of No. 13.	Shaka S. 1127 & 1131.	
14	Lakshmīdēva II ..	Mahāmaṇḍalēshvara.	Son of No. 13.	Shaka S. 1151.	

THE EARLY RĀSHṬRAKŪṬAS OF RĀJASTHĀNA (RĀJPŪTĀNĀ).

HASTIKUṆḌĪ (HATHŪṆḌĪ) BRANCH.

FROM ABOUT V.S. 950 (A.D. 893)
TO
ABOUT V.S. 1053 (A.D. 996.)

Traces of the existence of Rāshṭrakūṭa kingdoms at Hastikuṇḍī (Marwar) and Dhanōp (Shāhpurā) in Rājpūtānā are found even before the advent, to that province, of the descendants of the Gāhaḍavāla king Jayachchandra of Kanauj.

An inscription[1] of V.S. 1053 (A.D. 997) has been found at Bījāpur (Gōdwār district in the Marwar State), in which the genealogy of the Rāṭhōras of Hathūṇḍī is given as follows:—

1. HARIVARMAN.

The aforesaid genealogical table opens with this name.

2. VIDAGDHARĀJA.

He was the son of Harivarman and lived in V.S. 973=A.D. 916).[2]

3. MAMMAṬA.

He was the son of Vidagdharāja and seems to have lived in V.S. 996 (A.D. 939)[3].

---

1 Journal Bengal Asiatic Society, Vol. LXII, page 311.
2 Do. do. do. page 314.
3 Do. do. do. page 314.

4. DHAVALA.

He was the son of Mammaṭa and helped the ruler of Mēwār when Paramāra king Munja of Mālwā attacked him[1] and destroyed Āhāḍa.

He defended the Chauhāna chief Mahēndra of Nāḍōl from the attack of Chauhāna king Durlabharāja of Sāmbhar and protected king Dharaṇīvarāha from falling a prey to Sōlankī Mūlarāja king of Anhilwāḍā (Gujrāt). Dharaṇīvarāha, the ruler of Mārwār, probably, belonged to the Pratihāra dynasty. The aforesaid inscription of V.S. 1053 (A.D. 997) belongs to this king (Dhavala).[2]

In his old age king Dhavala made over the reins of the government to his son Bālaprasāda about V.S. 1053. His capital was Hastikuṇḍī (Hathūṇḍī).

As no inscription, etc., of a later date of this family has been traced, its further history is yet unknown.

THE GENEALOGICAL TABLE OF THE EARLY RĀṬHŌRAS OF Hastikuṇḍī.

1. Harivarman.
2. Vidagdharāja.
3. Mammaṭa.
4. Dhavala.
5. Bālaprasāda.

STATEMENT GIVING PARTICULARS OF THE EARLY RĀṬHŌRAS OF HASTIKUṆḌĪ.

No.	Name.	Relation.	Dates.	Contemporaries.
1	Harivarman ..			
2	Vidagdharāja ..	Son of No. 1.	V.S. 973.	
3	Mammaṭa ..	Do. 2.	V.S. 996.	
4	Dhavala.. ..	Do. 3.	V.S. 1053.	Paramāra Munja, Chauhāna Durlabharāja, Chauhāna Mahēndra, Sōlankī Mūlarāja and Pratihāra Dharaṇīvarāha.
5	Bālaprasāda ..	Do. 4.		

1 Probably Mahālakshmī, the sister of this king Dhavala, or of his father was married to Bhartribhaṭṭa II, the ruler of Mēwār, from whom Allaṭa was born.

2 King Dhavala repaired the Jain temple built by his grandfather Vidagdharāja and reinstalled therein the idol of Rishabhanātha.

THE EARLY RĀSHṬRAKŪṬAS OF DHANŌP (RĀJPŪTĀNĀ).

Sometime back two inscriptions of the Rāṭhōras were found at Dhanōp (Shāhpura) which are now untraceable. One of these was dated the 5th day of the bright half of 'Pausha', V.S. 1063, which showed that there was a king named Bhallīla of the Rāṭhōra dynasty and his son was Dantivarman. This Dantivarman had two sons:—Buddharāja and Gōvindarāja.

In the inscription of Shaka S. 788 (V.S. 923=A.D. 866) of king Amōghavarsha I, found at Nilgund in the Bombay Presidency, it is stated that his father, king Gōvindarāja III, had conquered the rulers of Kērala, Mālava, Gauḍa, Gurjara, Chitrakūṭa (Chittor) and Kānchī. This shows that the Rāṭhōras of Hastikūṇḍī and Dhanōp might be the offshoots of the Rāshṭrakuṭas of the Deccan.

THE GENEALOGICAL TABLE OF THE EARLY RĀṬHŌRAS OF DHANŌP.

Bhallīla.
|
Dantivarman.
|
Buddharāja. — Gōvindarāja.

THE GĀHAḌAVĀLAS OF KANAUJ.

FROM ABOUT V.S. 1125 (A.D 1068)
TO
ABOUT V.S. 1280 (A.D. 1223).

Col. James Tod has stated in his 'Annals of Rājasthāna' that in V.S. 526 (A.D. 470) Rāṭhōra Nayapāla acquired the kingdom of Kanauj after killing king Ajayapāla.[1] This assertion does not seem to be correct, for, though the Rāshṭrakūṭas had had their sway over Kanauj ere this, yet about this particular period king Skandagupta or his son Kumāragupta of the Imperial Gupta dynasty ruled over Kanauj[2]. After this, the Maukharīs occupied it,[3] and their power was set aside, for some time, by the Baisas, who took possession of Kanauj[4]. But after the death of Harsha the Maukharīs again made it their capital. About V.S. 798 (A.D. 741) king Lalitāditya (Muktāpīḍa) of Kāshmīr invaded Kanauj, which then too was the capital of Yashōvarman, the Maukharī ruler[5]. Further it appears from the copper grant[6] of V.S. 1084 (A.D. 1027) of Pratihāra king Trilōchanapāla and from the inscription[7] of V.S. 1093 (A.D. 1036) of Yashahpāla that the Pratihāras ruled over Kanauj about that time.

---

1 Annals and Antiquities of Rājasthān, (Ed. by W. Crooke) page 930.
2 Bhārata-kē-Prāchīna Rajavamsha, part II, pages 285-297.
3 Do. do. do. page 373.
4 Do. do. do. page 338.
5 Do. do. do. page 376.
6 Indian Antiquary, Vol. XVIII, page 34.
7 Asiatic Researches, Vol. IX, page 432.

Later, Rāshṭrakūṭa[1] Chandradēva (whose descendants were afterwards known as Gāhaḍavālas owing to their sway over Gādhipur, *i.e.*, Kanauj), having conquered Badāūn about V.S. 1111 (A.D. 1054), took possession of Kanauj. Thus, the kingdom of Kanauj once more came into the possession of the Rāshṭrakūṭas.[2]

About 70 copper grants and inscriptions of these Gāhaḍavālas have been found in which they are mentioned as 'Sūryavamshīs'. But the mention of the Gahāḍavāla dynasty is only found in three grants of V.S. 1161, 1162 and 1166 issued by Gōvindachandra while he was a prince regent as well as in the inscription of his queen Kumāradēvī. Further, there is no mention of the word Rāshṭrakūṭa or Raṭṭa in them, but they belonged to a branch of the Rāshṭrakūṭas as has been separately discussed elsewhere.[3] The Gāhaḍavālas had their sway over Kāshī (Benares), Oudh, and, perhaps, over Indrasthāna (Delhi) too[4].

1. YASHŌVIGRAHA.

He is known to be a descendant of the Sōlar dynasty. This is the first name traceable of this family.

2. MAHĪCHANDRA.

Also known as Mahiyala, Mahiala or Mahītala, was the son of Yashōvigraha.

---

1 Journal Royal Asiatic Society of Great Britain and Ireland, January 1930, pages 115-119.

2 The kingdom of Rāshṭrakūṭa Dhruvarāja of the Deccan had extended in the north upto Ayōdhyā between V.S. 842-850; later, in the time of Kṛishṇarāja II, between V.S. 932 and 971, its frontier had reached near the bank of the Ganges. Further, between V.S. 997 and 1023, in Kṛishṇa III's time, it had extended even beyond the Ganges. Probably, at this time, a member of this dynasty or some survivor of the early Rāshṭrakūṭa rulers of Kanauj, might have received a 'Jāgīr' here, in whose family king Chandra, the conqueror of Kanauj, was born.

3 Journal Royal Asiatic Society, January 1930, pages 111-121.

4 V.A. Smith's Early History of India, page 384.

3. CHANDRADĒVA.

He was the son of Mahīchandra. Three copper grants, of this king, of V.S. 1148 (A.D. 1091), V.S. 1150[1] (A.D. 1093) and V.S. 1156 (A.D. 1100) have been found at Chandrāvatī[2].

From the copper grants of his descendants it appears that he made Kanauj his capital and put down the anarchy resulting from the deaths of Rājā Bhōja[3] of the Parmāra dynasty of Mālwā and Karṇa[4] of the Haihaya (Kalachurī) dynasty of Chēdī.

From his first grant, it is evident that he gained strength about V.S. 1111 (A.D. 1054) and afterwards seized the kingdom of Kanauj[5] from the Pratihāras.

This king made several charitable gifts of gold weighing equal to his person. The districts of Kāshī, Kushika (Kanauj), northern Kōshala (Oudh) and Indrasthāna (Delhi) were under his sway. He also built a 'Vaishṇava' temple of Ādikēshava at Kāshī.

A copper grant,[6] of V.S. 1154 (A.D. 1097), of his son Madanapāla has been found, which contains a mention

---

1 In the copper grant of V.S. 1150 there is a mention of Pratihāra Dēvapāla of Kanauj :—

"श्रीदेवपालनृपतिस्त्रिजगत्प्रतीत:"

An inscription of Dēvapāla dated V.S. 1005 (A.D. 948) has been found. (Epigraphia Indica, Vol. I, page 177).

2 Epigraphia Indica, Vol. IX, page 302, and Vol. XIV, pages 192-209.

3 याते श्रीभोजभूपे विबुधवरवधूनेत्रसीमातिथित्वं
श्रीकर्णे कीर्तिशेषं गतवति च नृपे क्ष्मात्यये जायमाने ।
भर्तारं यं व (ध) रित्री त्रिदिवविभुनिभं प्रीतियोगादुपेता
त्राता विश्वासपूर्वं समभवदिह स क्ष्मापतिश्चन्द्रदेव: ॥

i.e., being oppressed by the anarchy prevailing after the deaths of Rājās Bhōja and Karṇa, the earth sought refuge with Chandradēva.

King Bhōja mentioned here is supposed by some historians to be the Pratihāra Bhōja?

4 Bhārat-kē-Prāchīna Rājavaṃsha, Vol. I, page 50.

5 Some historians assign V.S. 1135 (A.D. 1078) to Chandradēva's conquest of Kanauj.

6 Indian Antiquary, Vol. XVIII, page 11.

of the charity, given by Chandradēva. This shows that, though Chandra was alive upto that date, he had made over the reins of the Government to his son Madanapāla. The following are the titles attached to Chandra's name:—Paramabhaṭṭāraka, Mahārājādhirāja, Paramēshvara and Parama Māhēshvara. Chandrāditya appears as a second name of this king.

He had two sons:—Madanapāla and Vigrahapāla. from this Vigrahapāla, probably, the Badāūn family took its origin.

4. MADANAPĀLA.

He was the eldest son and successor of Chandradēva. Five copper grants of the time of Madanapāla have been found, the first being the aforesaid one of V.S. 1154[1] (A.D. 1097).

The second,[2] of V.S. 1161 (A.D. 1104), is of his son (Mahārājaputra) Gōvindachandra, in which there is a mention of the charitable grant of the village "Basāhī" together with the cess called "Turushkadaṇḍa." This shows that just as "Jaziā" was levied upon the Hindūs this 'Turushkadaṇḍa' was levied by Madanapāla upon the Mohammedans. Further, this is the first grant in which the word 'Gahaḍavāla' is mentioned.

The third,[3] of V.S. 1162 (A.D. 1105), is also of the Mahārājaputra Gōvindachandra and mentions the name of the senior queen of Madanapāla and mother of Gōvindachandra as Rālhadēvī.[4] (This too contains the mention of the word Gahaḍavāla.)

The fourth[5] is of V.S. 1163 (in fact of 1164) (A.D. 1107). This is of king Madanapāla himself, in which his queen's name appears as Pṛithvīshrīkā.

---

1 Indian Antiquary, Vol. XVIII, page 11.
2 Do. do. XIV, page 103.
3 Epigraphia Indica, Vol. II, page 359.
4 She was also called Rālhaṇadēvī.
5 Journal Royal Asiatic Society, (1896), page 787.

The fifth,[1] of V.S. 1166 (A.D. 1109), is also of Mahārājaputra Gōvindachandradēva. (In which also it is stated that he belonged to the Gahaḍavāla clan.)

Madanadēva was the second name of the king. His titles were:—Parama Bhaṭṭāraka, Paramēshvara, Parama Māhēshvara and Mahārājādhirāja. He had gained victories in many a battle. From the aforesaid copper grants it appears that Madanapāla, too, in his old age made over the government to his son Gōvindachandra.

THE SILVER COINS[2] OF MADNAPĀLA.

On the obverse there is an image of a horseman along with some illegible letters. On the reverse there is an image of a bull with the legend "Mādhava Shrī Sāmanta" along the border. The diameter of these coins is a bit smaller than ½ an inch and they are made of base silver.

THE COPPER COINS[3] OF MADANAPĀLA.

On the obverse of these, too, there is a rude image of a horseman and the legend "Madanapāladēva." On the reverse, like the silver coins, there is an image of a bull and the legend "Mādhava Shrī Sāmanta". They are a bit bigger than ½ an inch in diameter.

5. GŌVINDACHANDRA.

He was the eldest son and successor of Madanapāla. 42 copper plates and 2 inscriptions of his reign have been discovered, of which the first, second and third copper grants of V.S. 1161 (A.D. 1104), 1162 (A.D. 1105), and 1166 (A.D. 1109)[4] respectively, have already been mentioned in his father's history. As till then he

1 Indian Antiquary, Vol. XVIII, page 15.

2 Catalogue of the coins in the Indian Museum, Calcutta, Vol. I, page 260.

3 Catalogue of the coins in the Indian Museum, Calcutta, Vol. I, page 260, plate 26, No. 17.

4 It shows that Gōvindachandra defeated the "Gauḍa" and that the "Hammīrs" (Mohammedans) were also awe-struck by his bravery.

was regarded a prince his reign might have commenced from V.S. 1167 (A.D. 1110).

The fourth, fifth and sixth copper plates[1] are of V.S. 1171 (A.D. 1114). Of the fourth, only the first plate has been found, *i.e*, it is incomplete. The seventh[2] is of V.S. 1172 (A.D. 1116). The eighth[3] of V.S. 1174 (A.D. 1117) was issued from Dēvasthāna and contains a mention of his army of elephants. The ninth[4] is also of V.S. 1174 (in fact of 1175) (A.D. 1119) and the tenth[5] of V.S. 1175 (A.D. 1119). The eleventh, twelfth and thirteenth[6] of V.S. 1176 (A.D. 1119) were issued from the village Khayarā on the Ganges, Mumdaliya and Benares respectively. The eleventh contains the name of his senior queen Nayanakēlidēvī. The fourteenth[7] and fifteenth[8] are of 1177 (A.D. 1120) and the sixteenth[9] of V.S. 1178 A.D. 1122).

The seventeenth[10] plate of V.S. 1180 (A.D. 1123) contains along with the king's other titles, the decorations 'Ashvapati', 'Gajapati', 'Narapati', 'Rājatrayādhipati', Vividhavidyāvichāravāchaspati', etc. The eighteenth[11] of V.S. 1181 (A.D. 1124) contains his mother's name "Rālhaṇadēvī." The ninteenth[12] of V.S. 1182 (A.D. 1125) was issued from the place "Madapratīhāra" on the Ganges. The twentieth[13] of V.S. 1182

1 List of Northern (Indian) inscriptions, No. 692; Epigraphia Indica, Vol. IV, page 102 and Vol. VIII, page 153. The second was issued from Benāres.

2 Epigraphia Indica, Vol. IV, page 104.

3 Do. do. do. 105.

4 Indian Antiquary, Vol XVIII, page 19.

5 Epigraphia Indica, Vol. IV, page 106.

6 Epigraphia Indica, Vol. IV, page 108, Vol. XVIII, page 220 and Vol. IV, page 109.

7 Journal Bengal Asiatic Society, Vol. XXXI, page 123.

8 Epigraphia Indica, Vol. XVIII, page 225.

9 Epigraphia Indica, Vol. IV, page 110.

10 Journal Bengal Asiatic Society, Vol. LVI, page 108. (Dr. Bhandarkar gives the date as V.S. 1187.)

11 Journal Bengal Asiatic Society, Vol. LVI, page 114.

12 Epigraphia Indica, Vol. IV, page 100.

13 Journal Bengal Asiatic Society, Vol. XXVII, page 242.

(A.D. 1127) (originally of V.S. 1183) was issued from the village "Īshapratisṭhāna" on the Ganges. The twenty-first and twenty-second plates[1] are of V.S. 1183 (A.D. 1123) and V.S. 1184 (A.D. 1127) respectively.

The twenty-third plate[2] is of V.S. 1185 (A.D. 1129).

The twenty-fourth and twenty-fifth plates[3] are of V.S. 1186 (A.D. 1130).

The twenty-sixth plate[4] is of V.S. 1187 (A.D. 1130).

The twenty-seventh plate[5] is of V.S. 1188 (A.D. 1131).

The twenty-eighth plate[6] is of V.S. 1189 (A.D. 1133).

The twenty-ninth and thirtieth plates[7] are of V.S. 1190 (A.D. 1133).

The thirty-first plate[8] is of V.S. 1191 (A.D. 1134), of Mahārājaputra Vatsrājadēva of the "Singara" family, who was a feudatory of king Gōvindachandra and was also called "Lōhaḍadēva".

The thirty-second[9] and the thirty-third[10] plates are of V.S. 1196(A.D. 1139) and V.S. 1197 (A.D. 1141) respectively. The thirty-fourth[11] of V.S. 1198 (A.D. 1141) speaks of a charitable grant made on the occasion of the first anniversary of his senior queen Rālhadēvi's demise.

The thirty-fifth[12] plate of V.S. 1199 (A.D. 1143) contains a mention of the king's (Gōvindachandra's) son Mahārājaputra Rājyapāladeva.[13] The thirty-sixth,[14] thirty-seveth[15] and thirty-eighth[16] plates are of V.S. 1200

---

1 Journal Bihar and Orissa reasearch Society, Vol. II, page 445 and Epigraphia Indica, Vol. IV, page 111.
2 Journal Bengal Asiatic Society, Vol. LVI, page 119.
3 Lucknow Museum Report of 1914-15, pages 4-10, Epigraphia Indica, Vol. XIII, page 297 and Vol. XI, page 22.
4 Epigraphia Indica, Vol. VIII, page 153.
5 Indian Antiquary, Vol. XIX, page 249.
6 Epigraphia Indica, Vol. V, page 114.
7 Epigraphia Indica, Vol. VIII, page 155 and Vol. IV, page 112.
8 Epigraphia Indica, Vol. IV, page 131.
9 Epigraphia Indica, Vol. II, page 361.
10 Epigraphia Indica, Vol. IV, page 114.
11 Epigraphia Indica, Vol. IV, page 113.
12 Indian Antiquary, Vol. XVIII, page 21.
13 He was born of Nayanakēlidēvī and might have predeceased his father.
14 Epigraphia Indica, Vol. IV, page 115.
15 Epigraphia Indica, Vol. V, page 115.
16 Epigraphia Indica, Vol. VII, page 99.

(A.D. 1144), V.S. 1201 (A.D 1146) and V.S. 1202 (A.D. 1146) respectively. The thirty-ninth[1] and fortieth[2] plates are of V.S. 1203 (A.D. 1146) and V.S. 1207 (A.D. 1150). A stone pillar inscription[3] of V.S. 1207 (A.D. 1151) of this king has been found at Hāthiyadah in which the name of his queen is mentioned as Gōsalladēvī.

The forty-first[4] copper grant of Gōvindachandra, of V.S. 1208 (A.D. 1151), contains a mention of the charitable grant made by his senior queen Gōsaladēvī, who is described as enjoying all the honours of the state. The forty-second plate[5] is of V.S. 1211 (A.D. 1154).

An inscription[6] of Gōvindachandra's queen Kumāradēvī,[7] daughter of king Dēvarakshita of the Chikkōra dynasty of Pīṭhikā, was found at Sārnāth, which shows that this queen had built a temple and had dedicated it to Dharmachakra Jina.

Looking to the vast number of the copper grants of Gōvindachandra, we understand that he was a powerful and generous ruler and most probably for some time he was the greatest king in Northern India and had retained his sway over Benāres[8].

---

1 Epigraphia Indica, Vol. VIII, page 157.

2 Epigraphia Indica, Vol. VIII, page 159.

3 Archaeological Survey of India report Vol. I, page 96.

4 Kielhorn's list of inscriptions of N. I., page 19, No. 131.

5 Epigraphia Indica, Vol. IV, page 116.

6 Epigraphia Indica, Vol. IX, pages 319-328.

7 This Kumāradēvī was a follower of Buddhism. In a manuscript copy of the book entitled 'Ashṭasārikā' preserved in the Nēpāl State library, it is thus stated:—

"श्रीमद्गोविन्दचन्द्रदेवप्रतापवशात: राज्ञी श्रीप्रवरमहायानयायिन्या:
परमोपासिका राज्ञी वसन्तदेवी देयधर्मोऽयम्"

This shows that Gōvindachandra's another queen Vasantadēvī, too, was a follower of the Mahāyāna branch of Buddhism. Some people hold Vasantadēvī to be another name of Kumāradēvī. In the 'Rāmacharita' written by Sandhyākaranandī, king Mahaṇa (Mathana), father of Kumāradēvī's mother is stated to be of the Rāshṭrakūṭa dynasty.

8 Of the 21 copper grants found near Benares 14 belong to this king Gōvindachandra.

He had sent out Suhala, as his delegate, to the great convocation called by Alankāra, the minister of king Jayasimha, of Kāshmīr. This fact is stated in the 'Shrīkanṭhacharitakāvya' of poet Mankha:—

अन्यः स सुहलस्तेन ततोऽवन्द्यत पण्डितः ।
दूतोगोविन्दचन्द्रस्य कान्यकुब्जस्य भूभुजः ॥ १०२ ॥

(श्रीकण्ठचरितम्, सर्ग २५)

i.e., he offered his respects to the great scholar Suhala, the delegate of the king Gōvindachandra of Kanauj.

This Gōvindachandra had also fought with the Mohammedan (Turk) invaders of India[1] and had conquered the provinces of Gauḍa and Chēdi. From the decoration "Vividhavidyāvichāravāchaspati" attached to his name we understand that, besides being a patron of learning, he himself was a good scholar.

Under his orders his minister Lakshmīdhara, compiled a book on law entitled "Vyavahārakalpataru."

Names of his three sons are found as below:— Vijayachandra, Rājyapāla and Āsphōtachandra.

Mr. V. A. Smith holds the period of Gōvindachandra's reign to be from A.D. 1104 to 1155 (V.S. 1161 to 1212).[2] But it is quite clear that his father was alive upto V.S. 1166 (A.D. 1109), hence upto that date he was only a prince regent.

Many gold and copper coins of Govindachandra have been found. Though the metal of the gold coins is rather debased, they are found in abundance. Eight hundred of these were found at the village Nānpāra (Behraich, Oudh) in V.S. 1944 (A.D. 1887) when the Bengal North-Western Railway was under construction.

---

1 Perhaps, these were the Turks that were then making advances from the Lahore side.

2 Early history of India, (Fourth edition), page 400.

THE GOLD COINS[1] OF GŌVINDACHANDRA.

On the obverse there are three lines of the legend. The first line reads 'श्रीमद्गो', the second 'विन्दचन्द्र' and the third "देव". There is also a trident in the third line, which is probably a mark of the mint. On the reverse there is a rude image of the Goddess Lakshmī in the sitting posture. These are a bit larger in size than the current British Indian silver four anna piece.

THE COPPER COINS[2] OF GŌVINDACHANDRA.

On the obverse there are two lines of writing. The first contains "श्रीमद्गो" and the second "विन्दचन्द्र". On the reverse there is a very rude image of the Goddess Lakshmī in the sitting posture. These coins are rare and are about the size of the British Indian silver four anna piece.

6. VIJAYACHANDRA.

He was the son and successor of Gōvindachandra and was also known as Malladēva.[3] Two copper grants and two inscriptions of this king have been found. The first copper plate[4] is of V.S. 1224 (A.D. 1168) in which the king's title is mentioned as Mahārājādhirāja, and that of his son Jayachchandradēva, as Yuvarāja (prince regent). There is also a mention of Vijayachandra's victory[5] over the Mohammedans. The second[6] copper grant of V.S. 1225 (A.D. 1169) also contains a mention of the king as well as of his heir-apparent in the same manner as the first.

---

1 Catalogue of the coins in the Indian Museum, Calcutta, Vol. I, pages 260-261, plate 26, No. 18.

2 Catalogue of the coins in the Indian Museum, Calcutta, Vol. I, page 261.

3 "Rambhāmanjarī Nātikā," page 6.

4 Epigraphia Indica, Vol. IV, page 118.

5 भुवनदलनहेलाहर्म्यहम्मीरनारीनयनजलदधाराधौतभूतोपतापः"

This shows that he might have fought with Khusrō of Ghaznī, who at that time, had settled at Lahore.

6 Indian Antiquary, Vol, XV, page 7.

The first inscription[1] is of V.S. 1225 (A.D. 1169). It does not contain the name of his son. The second inscription,[2] which is dated V.S. 1225 (A.D. 1169), belongs to the commander-in-chief, Pratāpadhavala, and contains the mention of a forged copper grant of Vijayachandra.

The king was a follower of Vaishṇavism and built many temples[3] of Vishṇu. His queen's name was Chandralēkhā. He invested his son, Jayachchandra, with the powers of administration during his lifetime. His army consisted of a large number of elephants and horses. In the inscription of Jayachchandra this king is mentioned as a victor of the world. But in the inscription[4] of V.S. 1220 of Chauhāna Vigraharāja IV there is a mention of his (Vigraharāja's) victory from which it follows that if Vijayachandra had conquered any country he might have done so before this date.

In the 'Pṛithvīrāja Rāso' Vijayachandra is named as Vijayapāla.

JAYACHCHANDRA.

He was the son and successor of Vijayachandra. On the day of his birth his grandfather, Govindachandra, had gained a victory over Dashārṇa country, to commemorate which, the then born grand heir to the throne was named Jaitrachandra[5] (Jayantachandra or Jayachchandra).

---

1 Archaelogical Survey of India, (report), Vol. XI, page 125.
2 Journal American Oriental Society, Vol. VI, page 548.
3 The ruins of these temples are still existent in Jaunpur.
4 Bhārata-kē-Prāchīna Rājavamsha, Vol. I, page 244.

5 " आओ जम्मि दिणम्मि एस सुकिदी चन्दे जुए भीइणा
पत्तं तम्मि दसण्णगेसु पबलं जं खप्पराणं बलं ।
जित्तं झत्ति पियामहेण पहुणा जैतंति नामं तओ
दिन्नं जस्स स अज्ज वेरिदलणो दिट्ठो जयंतप्पहू ॥"

संस्कृतच्छाया—

"जातो यस्मिन् दिने एष सुकृती चन्द्रे युते अभिजिता
प्राप्तं तस्मिन् दशार्णकेषु प्रबलं यत् खर्पराणां बलम् ।
जितं झटिति पितामहेन प्रभुणा जैत्रेति नाम ततः
दत्तं यस्य स अद्य वैरिदलनः दृष्टः जैत्रप्रभुः "
....
श्री भरतकुलप्रदीपश्रीजैत्रचन्द्रनरेश्वराय...

(रम्भामञ्जरी नाटिका, पृ० २३-२४)

From the aforesaid copper grant of V.S. 1224, of king Vijayachandra, it is evident that Jayachchandra had been invested with ruling powers during his father's life-time.

In the preface to the drama named 'Rambhāmanjarī Nātikā',[1] by Nayachandra Sūri, it is thus stated:—

"अभिनवरामावतारश्रीमन्मदनवर्ममेदिनीदयितसाम्राज्यलक्ष्मीकरेणुकालानस्त-म्भायमानबाहुदण्डस्य"

i.e., whose (Jayachchandra's) mighty arm is like a pillar to tether the elephant of fortune of king Madanavarmadēva.

This shows that Jayachchandra probably had extended his sway over Kālinjar and defeated its king Madanavarmadēva[2] of the Chandēla dynasty. Similarly, having defeated the Bhōrs, he also annexed Khōr.

Fourteen copper grants and two inscriptions of his reign have been found.

The first[3] copper plate is of V.S. 1226 (A.D. 1170) granted from the village Vaḍaviha. It contains an account of the Rājyābhishēka (Coronation) of the king, which was performed on Sunday, the sixth day of the bright half of Āshāḍha, V.S. 1226 (21st June, 1170 A.D.).

The second[4] plate is of V.S. 1228 (A.D. 1172) issued from the Trivēṇi confluence (Allahabad). The third[5] is of V.S. 1230 (A.D. 1173) issued from Vārāṇasī (Benāres).

The fourth[6] is of V.S. 1231 (A.D. 1174) issued from Kāshī (Benares). From the thirty-second line of this plate it appears that this copper grant was engraved later in V.S. 1235 (A.D. 1179). The fifth[7] plate is of

1 Page 4.
2 His last grant is of V.S. 1219 (A.D. 1183) and that of his successor Paramardidēva of V. S. 1223 (A.D. 1167). This shows that the victory mentioned above was gained by Jayachchandra while he was a prince regent.
3 Epigraphia Indica, Vol. IV, page 121.
4 Epigraphia Indica, Vol. IV, page 122.
5 Do. do. do. 124.
6 Do. do. do. 125.
7 Do. do. do. 127.

V.S. 1232 (A.D. 1175) and contains the name of the king's son, Harishchandra, at whose 'Jātakarma' ceremony the charity mentioned was granted from Benāres. From the thirty-first and thirty-second lines of this plate, too, we infer that the plate was actually prepared like the preceding one in V.S. 1235 (A.D. 1179).

The sixth copper plate[1] is of V.S. 1232 (A.D. 1175). The charity mentioned therein was granted on the occasion of the naming ceremony of Harishchandra. The seventh[2], the eighth[3] and the ninth[4] plates are of V.S. 1233 (A.D. 1177) and the tenth[5] is of V.S. 1234 (A.D. 1177). The eleventh,[6] the twelth[7] and the thirteenth[8] are all of V.S. 1236 (A.D. 1180). These three were issued at the village of Raṇḍavai situated on the Ganges. The fourteenth[9] plate is of V.S. 1243 (A.D. 1187). The first inscription[10] of V.S. 1245 (A.D. 1189) of this king has been found at Meohaḍ (near Allahabad) and the second inscription[11] at Buddha Gayā, which is a Buddhist inscription and contains a mention of this king. The fourth digit of the number indicating the year of this inscription being spoiled, it reads 124— only.

This king was a very powerful monarch and had so immense an army that people called him by the nickname 'Dalapangula'[12].

---

1 Indian Antiquary, Vol. XVIII, page 130.
2 Epigraphia Indica, Vol. IV, page 129.
3 Indian Antiquary, Vol. XVIII, page 135.
4 Do. do. do. 137.
5 Do. do. do. 138.
6 Do. do. do. 140.
7 Do. do. do. 141.
8 Do. do. do. 142.
9 Do. do. XV, 10.

10 Annual report of the Archaeological Survey of India, (A.D. 1921-22), pages 120-121.

11 Proceedings of the Bengal Asiatic Society, (1880), page 77.

12 "अप्रतिमल्लप्रतापस्य श्रीमन्मल्लदेवतनुजन्मनः सतीमल्लिका-
श्रीचन्द्रलेखाकुक्षिशुक्तिमुक्तामणेः गङ्गायमुनास्रोतस्विनीयष्टिद्वयमन्तरेण
रिपुमेदिनीदयितदत्तदैन्यसैन्यसागरवरं प्रचालयितुमक्षमत्वात्
पंगुरिति प्राप्तगुरुविरुदस्य श्रीमज्जैत्रचन्द्रनरेश्वरस्य"

(रम्भामञ्जरी नाटिका, पृ. ६)

i.e., who has earned the title of "Pangu" (lame) being unable to mobilize his immense armies without the support of two sticks—Gangā and Yamunā. It is also evident from the above reference that the title of Jayachchandra's father was Malladēva and the name of his mother was Chandralēkhā.

Poet Shri Harsha, the author of the famous poem 'Naishadhīya Charita,' also flourished in his court. The name of this poet's mother was Māmalladēvī and that of his father Hīra, as appears from the concluding stanzas of each of the chapters of the aforesaid poem running as follows:—

'श्रीहर्षं कविराजराजिमुकुटालङ्कारहीरः सुतं
श्रीहीरः सुषुवे जितेन्द्रियचयं मामल्लदेवी च यम् ॥'

i.e., Hīra begot Harsha in Māmalladēvī.

In the conclusion of this 'Naishadhīya Charita' it is thus stated:—

'ताम्बूलद्वयमासनं च लभते यः कान्यकुब्जेश्वरात् ।'

i.e., in the court of the king of Kanauj Shrī Harsha had the privilege of being seated on an "Āsana" and of being honoured with the offer of a betel (ताम्बूल) on attending and leaving the court.

Though there is no mention of Jayachchandra in 'Naishadhīya Charita,' yet from the 'Prabandha Kōsha' compiled by Rājashēkhara Sūri, in V.S. 1405, we learn that this poet flourished in the court of this king.

This Shrī Harsha had also written the book named "Khaṇḍanakhaṇḍakhādya." It is thus stated in the end of the 'Dvirūpakōsha":—

इत्थं श्रीकविराजराजमुकुटालङ्कारहीरार्पित-
श्रीहीरात्मभवेन नैषधमहाकाव्ये ज्वलत्कीर्तिना ।
औद्धत्यप्रतिवादिमत्तकटीविन्यस्तवामांघ्रिणा
श्रीहर्षेण कृतो द्विरूपविलसत्कोशस्सतां श्रेयसे ॥

It shows that thīs book (Dvirūpakōsha) was also written by the same poet.

Jayachchandra was the last powerful Hindū monarch of Kanauj. According to 'Prithvīrāja Rāsō' he had performed the great sacrifice called "Rājasūya Yagya" and the 'Svayamvara' ceremony of his daughter Samyōgitā, which brought about the downfall of the Hindu Empire in India. In this

'Svayamvara' as Prithvīrāja, the Chauhāna king of Delhi, forcibly abducted and married the princess, enmity broke out between the two most powerful kings of India (Jayachchandra and Prithvīrāja). This internal discord afforded a golden opportunity to Shahābuddīn to invade India. But the story of the "Rāsō" is a mere fiction, as firstly there is no mention of 'Rājasūya' or the 'Svayamvara' of Samyōgita in the grants or inscriptions of Jayachchandra, secondly no trace of the abduction of Samyōgitā is found in the poems connected with Chauhāna Prithvīrāja, and thirdly 'Prithvīrāja Rāsō' records the death of Mahārāvala Samara Simha of Mēwār while helping Prithvīrāja against Shahābuddīn, but, in fact, he died 110 years after this event. We have fully discussed the subject in the appendix.

Shahābuddīn Ghōrī defeated Jayachchandra in the battle of Chandāval[1] (Etawah district) in A.H. 590 (V.S. 1250=A.D. 1194) and, in the plunder of Benāres, got so much wealth that 1400 camels were employed for its transport to Ghaznī[2].

From this period the Mohammedans acquired sovereignty in Northern India and, being dismayed by this defeat, Jayachchandra drowned himself in the Ganges. But anyhow for some time Kanauj remained under the possession of Harishchandra, the son of Jayachchandra.

The Mohammedan historians have mentioned Jayachchandra as the king of Benāres[3], which probably was the seat of his Government at that time.

---

1 'Tabqāt-i-Nāsirī, page 140.

2 'Kāmiluttavārīkh' (Elliot's translation) Vol. II, page 251.

3 In the Persian Chronicle, 'Tāju-Ma-āsir', written by Hasan Nizāmī, this event is thus described:—

After taking possession of Delhi next year Qutubuddīn Aibak invaded Kanauj. On the way Sultān Shahābuddīn also joined him. The invading army consisted of 50,000 horse. The Sultān posted Qutubuddīn in the vanguard. Jayachchandra met this army at Chandāval near Etawah. At the time of the battle king Jayachchandra, seated on an elephant, guided his forces, but was eventually killed. The Sultan's army then plundered the treasure of the fort of Āsnī and, having proceeded further, similarly took Benāres. He also got 300 elephants in this plunder.

Maulānā Minhājuddīn in his 'Tabqāt-i-Nāsirī' says that the two generals Qutubuddīn and Īzzuddīn accompanied the Sultān (Shahābuddīn) and defeated king Jayachchandra of Benāres near Chandāval in A.H. 590 (V.S. 1250).

Jayachchandra had built several forts, out of which one was built at Kanauj on the bank of the Ganges, another at Asaī, on the Jumna (in Etawah district), and a third at Kurrā (Kaḍā).[1] At Etawah, on a mound, near the bank of the Jumna, there exist, to this day, some remains which are supposed by the local people to be the remains of Jayachchandra's fort.

It is stated in the 'Prabandha Kōsha' that king Jayachchandra had conquered 700 'Yōjana' (5600 miles) of land. His son's name was Mēghachandra. Jayachchandra's minister, Padmākara, on his return from Aṇahilpur, brought with him a beautiful widow named Suhavādēvī. Being smitten with her love Jayachchandra kept her as his concubine and from her a son was born. When this illegitimate son came of age, his mother requested the king to declare him his heir-apparent. But the king's minister, Vidyādhara, announced prince Mēghachandra to be the rightful heir. This offended Suhavādēvī. She sent her secret agent to the Sultān's court at Taxila (Panjab) and planned the invasion of Kanauj.[2] Though the minister Vidyādhara, having learnt of the conspiracy through his spies, had given timely information to the king, yet he did not give any credit to it. The minister, being thus aggrieved, plunged himself into the Ganges. Shortly afterwards the Sultān appeared with his army on the scene. The king marched out to encounter him and a desparate battle was fought between the two. But it is still a mystery whether the king was killed on the battlefield or plunged himself into the Ganges.

1 This place is in the Allahabad district on the bank of the Ganges. It is alleged that the remains of Jayachchandra's fort on one bank of the river and those of his brother Māṇikachandra's fort on the opposite bank are still existent. The peculiar burial ground of the place also tells the tale of a battle being fought there, in which the victorious Jayachchandra had destroyed a very large number of his Muslim foes.

2 Mērutunga, too, in his "Prabandhachintāmaṇi" discredits Suhavādēvī for calling the Mohammedans. This book was written in V.S. 1362 (A.D. 1305).

HARISHCHANDRA.

Harishchandra, son of Jayachchandra, was born on the 8th day of the dark half of Bhādrapada, V.S. 1232 (the 10th August 1175) and after the death of Jayachchandra succeeded to the throne of Kánauj in V.S. 1250 (A.D. 1193) at the age of 18.

It is generally believed that on the death of Jayachchandra the Mohammedans took possession of Kanauj. But in the Mohammedan chronicles of the time such as 'Tājul-Ma-āsir' and 'Tabqāt-i-nāsirī', etc., it is stated that after the battle of Chandāval the Mohammedan army went towards Prayāg and Benāres. They speak of Jayachchandra as the Rājā of Benāres. This clearly shows that, though Kanauj had been devastated by the Mohammedans and its power had declined, still for some years the descendants of Jayachchandra had a hold over the country around it. It was Shamsuddīn Altamash who, for the first time, completely destroyed the Gāhḍavāla kingdom after taking possession of Kanauj.

Though in 'Tabqāt-i-nāsirī' Kanauj has been included in the list of the cities conquered by Qutubuddīn and Shamsuddīn[1] both, yet it is a point worth consideration that when it was already conquered by Qutubuddīn, what led Shamsuddīn[2] to re-conquer it.

Of the aforesaid two copper plates,[3] of V.S. 1232, of king Jayachchandra, the first mentions that he granted the village of Vaḍēsar to his family priest on the occasion of the 'Jātakarma' ceremony of his son, prince Harishchandra. And the second refers to the

1 Tabqāt-i-nāsirī, p. 179.

2 In the time of this Altamash a Kshatriya hero named Bartū destroyed a number of Mohammedans in Oudh. [Tabqāt-i-nāsirī (English translation) pages 628-629].

3 The first of these two was found at the village of Kamauli in Benāres district (Epigraphia Indica, Vol. IV, page 127); and the second at the village of Sihvar, also in the same district, (Indian Antiquary, Vol. XVIII, page 130).

grant of two villages given to a Brāhmaṇa named Hṛishīkēsha on the occasion of Harishchandra's name giving ceremony, performed on the 13th day of the bright half of Bhādrapadā, V.S. 1232 (the 31st August, 1175). At this time the prince was only 21 days old.

One copper grant and one inscription of the time of Harishchandra have been found.

The copper grant[1] was issued on the 15th day of the bright half of Pausha, V.S. 1253 (A.D. 1196) in which his titles (which are similar to those of his forefathers are mentioned as follows:—Paramabhaṭṭaraka, Mahārājādhirāja, Paramēshvara, Prama Māhēshvara, Ashvapati, Gajapati, Narapati, Rājatrayādhipati, Vividhavidyāvichāravāchaspati, etc. This shows that though a large part of the kingdom had passed away from his possession yet he maintained his independence to some extent.

The inscription of this king, too, is of V.S. 1253, which was found at Bēlkhēḍā. Though the king's name is not mentioned in this inscription, yet from the words "कान्यकुब्जविजयराज्ये" mentioned in it Mr. R. D. Banerji and other scholars hold it to be of the time of Harischandra.

As stated above, on the death of Jayachchandra, in the battle with Sultān Shahābuddīn, his son Harishchandra became the ruler of the country around Kanauj, while his relatives went towards Khōr[2]

1 Epigraphia Indica, Vol. X, page 95.

In this copper plate the Samvat is stated both in figures and words. The first digit of the figure appears to have been made by erasing some other figure. Mr. R. D. Bānerji reads it as 1257 (Journal Bengal Asiatic Society, Vol. VII, page 762, No. 11). If this version be taken as correct then this grant should have been written three years after giving the village of Pamahī.

2 From the history of Rāmpur we learn that when Shamsuddīn had invaded Khōr, Jajapāla acknowledged his supremacy and remained there, but his brother Prahasta* (Baradāīsēna) fled to Mahuī † (in the Farrukhābād district), while some of their relatives escaped to Nēpāl. After a time the descendants of Jajapāla leaving Khōr settled in Usēt (in the Badāūn district). Probably Lakhanapāla†, too, at that time lived there in the capacity of a feudatory. Afterwards being chased by the Mohammedans there, they went towards Bilsad††. Later Rām Rāi (Rāmsahāya), a descendant of Jajapāla, found the state of Rāmpur in the Etah district. The Rāo

(Shamsābād)[1] (in the Farrukhābād district). But when the few districts that remained under the control of Harishchandra were also attacked by Sultān Shamsuddīn Altamash the sons of Harishchandra (Bardāīsēna)[2] took their abode first in Khōr then in Mahuī.

But, sometime after, the Mohammedans began their inroads in this district also, and Sīhā,[3] the younger son of Bardāīsēna, was obliged, therefore, to migrate to Mārwār.

It is already stated above that Harishchandra's sons had gone away towards Mahuī. Here, after sometime, his younger son, Sīhā, had built a fort[4]; but later, when this region began to be overrun by the Mohammedans, Sīhā with his elder brother[5] Sētarāma was obliged to migrate westward with the intention of the pilgrimage to Dvārakā and reached Mārwār.

---

of Khimsēpur in the Farrukhabad district also claims his descent from Jajapāla. Similary, the Chaudharis of Surjaī and Sarōḍhā (Mainpuri district) are known as the descendants of Jajapāla.

It is said that Māṇikachandra was a brother of Jayachchandra. The rulers of Māṇḍā and Bījāpur, states in the Mirzāpur district, as well as some other petty landholders of Ghāzīpur district, claim their descent from Gāḍaṇa, the son of Māṇikachandra.

*In the 'Pratāpagaḍha Nāmā', published in A.D. 1849, this prince is mentioned as Harasū. Perhaps Harasū and Prahasta are corrupted forms of Harishchandra.

†Epigraphia Indica, Vol. I, page 64.

††At some places the time of this event is given as V.S. 1280.

1 In V.S. 1270 Shamsuddīn converted the name of Khōr as Shamsābād after his own name.

2 Possibly Baradāīsēna may be a younger brother of Harishchandra.

3 In the history of Rāmpur Sīhā is stated as the grand son of Prahasta, but in the History of Mārwār his grandfather's name is stated as Baradāīsēna. It is, therefore, probable that both these are the surnames of Harishchandra. It is also possible that just as 'Dalapangula' was a title of Jayachchandra Baradāīsēna (Varadāyīsainya) might be that of Harishchandra.

4 Its ruins are still existent on the bank of the Ganges and are locally known as 'Sīhā Rāo-kā-Khēḍā.'

5 It is stated in "Ain-i-Akbarī" that Sīhā was the nephew of Jayachandra, who lived at Shamsābād and was also killed in the battle fought with Shahābuddīn at Kanauj. (Vol. II, page 507).

In the 'Annals and Antiquities of Rājasthāna' at one place Sīhā is stated as the son of Jayachandra (Vol. I, page 105) while at other as the nephew (Vol. II, page 930). But at the third place he and Sētarāma both are stated to be the grandsons of Jayachandra (Vol. II, page 940).

In the inscription of Sīhā, dated V.S. 1330, he is stated as the son of Sētarāma.

But if we take Sētarāma to be the elder brother and adoptive father of Sīhā, firstly the times assigned to Jayachchandra and Sīhā adjust themselves well, secondly the controversies arising by the mention of Sētarāma at one place as the brother and at other as the father of Sīhā would also be squared up.

STATEMENT GIVING PARTICULARS OF THE GĀHAḌAVĀLAS OF KANAUJ.

No.	Name.	Special Title.	Relation.	Known Dates.	Contemporaries.
1	Yashōvigraha ..		Born in Sōlar dynasty.		
2	Mahīchandra ..		Son of No. 1.		
3	Chandradēva ..	Mahārājādhirāja.	Do. 2.	V. S. 1148, 1150, 1156.	Became king after the death of Paramāra Bhōja and Haihaya Karṇa.
4	Madanapāla.. ..	Do.	Do. 3.	V. S. 1154, 1161, 1162, 1163, 1166.	
5	Gōvindachandra ..	Vividhavidyāvichāravāchaspati	Do. 4.	V. S. 1161, 1162, 1166, 1171, 1172, 1174, 1175, 1176, 1177, 1178, 1180? 1181, 1182, (1183), 1183, 1184, 1185, 1186, 1187, 1188, 1189, 1190, 1191, 1196, 1197, 1198, 1199, 1200, 1201, 1202, 1203, 1207, 1208, 1211.	
6	Vijayachandra ..	Mahārājādhirāja.	Do. 5.	V. S. 1224, 1225.	
7	Jayachchandra ..	Do.	Do. 6.	V. S. 1226, 1228, 1230, 1231, 1232, 1233. 1234, (1235,) 1236, 1243, 1245.	Chandēla Madanavarmadēva, Chauhāna Pṛithvirāja, and Shahābuddīn Ghōrī.
8	Harishchandra ..	Do.	Do. 7.	V. S. 1253.	

Genealogical tree of the Gāhaḍavāla family of Kanauj.

- Yashōvigraha.
  - Mahīchandra.
    - Chandradēva.
      - Madanapāla.
        - Gōvindachandra.
          - Vijayachandra.
            - Jayachchandra.
              - Harishchandra. (Prahasta or Baradāīsēna).
                - Sētarāma.
                - Sihā.
              - Jajapāla.
              - Mēghachandra.
            - Māṇikachandra.
          - Rājyapāla.
          - Āsphōtachandra.
      - Vigrahapāla (head of the Badāūn family).

APPENDIX.

FALSE STATEMENTS ABOUT KING JAYACHCHANDRA AND RĀO SĪHĀ.[1]

Jayachchandra, king of Kanauj, has often been accused of having caused the downfall of the last Hindū kingdom in Northern India. His grandson Rāo Sīhā also has been accused of having usurped Pālī by treacherously murdering the Pallivāl Brāhmaṇas of that place. No reasons are, however, offered for these suppositions, but the only argument resorted to by these critics, is that these stories are handed down from generation to generation or that they are so mentioned in the "Pṛithvīrāja Rāsō" and in Tod's "Annals and Antiquities of Rājasthāna."

In fact, none has yet taken the trouble of investigating the truth or otherwise of the problem. For the consideration of scholars, I lay down my views on the subject here. The brief story of the "Pṛithvīrāja Rāsō" may be told as follows.

Once Kamadhaja Rāi, with the assistance of king Vijaypāla Rāhṭhōḍa of Kanauj invaded Delhi. At this, Tunvara Anangapāla, king of Delhi, requested king Sōmēshvara Chauhāna of Ajmer for help. Sōmēshvara thereupon marched with all his forces and joined Anangapāla. A battle was fought in which the latter won a victory, and the hostile forces retreated. As a mark of gratitude for this timely succour, Anangapāla married his younger daughter

Kamalāvatī to Somēshvara and simultaneously his another daughter[1] to Vijayapāla of Kanauj.

In V.S. 1115 Kamalāvatī gave birth to Pṛithvīrāja. Once Nāhaḍa Rāo, king of Maṇḍōr, had paid a visit to king Anangapāla of Delhi, and beholding the handsome features of prince Pṛithvīrāja there, he declared his intention to marry his daughter to him. But later, he abandoned the idea. On this Pṛithvīrāja invaded Maṇḍor in about V. S. 1129, and having defeated Nāhaḍa Rāo, took his daughter in marriage. Later, in V.S. 1138, Anangapāla, disregarding the right of his elder daughter's son Jayachchandra, made over the kingdom of Delhi to Pṛithvīrāja. Subsequently, Pṛithvīrāja having abducted the daughter of the Yādava king Bhaṇa of Deogiri, who was engaged to Vīrachandra, nephew of Jayachchandra, the armies of Pṛithvīrāja and Jayachchandra had to meet on the battle-field. Sometime after this, Anangapāla also invaded Delhi to recapture it from Pṛithvīrāja, on the complaints of his former subjects being now oppressed by Pṛithvīrāja's coercive policy, but he did not succeed.

In V.S. 1144, when Jayachchandra proposed to perform a 'Rājasūya-yajna' and the 'Svayamvara' of his daughter Samyogitā, Pṛithvīrāja, considering it inadvisable to confront him, thought out another plan to render both the above ceremonies abortive. He at first repaired to Khokhandapura where he killed Jayachchandra's brother, Bāluka Rāi, and afterwards eloped with Samyogīta. Jayachchandra was, therefore, obliged to wage war against Pṛithvīrāja. The latter managed somehow to escape, but as many as 64 of his generals were killed and his power was almost annihilated. According to the 'Rāso,' Pṛithvīrāja was 36 years of age when this event took place. So the date of the event must be Vikrama Samvat 1151.

---

1 Jayachchandra was born to this lady.

The bravery of the young general Dhīrasēna Pundīra in the struggle with Jayachchandra attracted Pṛithvīrāja's attention, and the king favoured him most. At this, his veteran generals Chāmuṇda Rāi and others became jealous and carried on intrigues with Shahābuddīn. But Pṛithvīrāja, being too much engrossed with Samyogīta, did not pay any heed to these affairs. His government, therefore, gradually showed signs of disintegration. This gave an opportunity to Shahābuddīn to invade Delhi. Pṛithvīrāja was obliged to come out with his army to meet him. On this occasion, Rāvala Samarasī of Mēwāṛ, his brother-in-law, had also joined Pṛithvīrāja in the battle. But due to disorganisation of the army, Shahābuddīn eventually won a victory, and Pṛithvīrāja was captured and taken to Ghaznī. Shortly after this, it is related, Shahābuddīn met his death at the hands of Pṛithvīrāja at Ghaznī, who immediately after killed himself.[1] Shortly after, Raiṇasī, son of Pṛithvīrāja, attacked the Muhammedans of Lahore, to avenge his father's death, and drove them out. Thereupon Qutbuddīn marched against Raiṇasī and killing him in the battle that followed, advanced further upon Kanauj. Hearing of this, Jayachchandra also arranged his army to encounter him. But in the battle that ensued, Jayachchandra was killed and the Muhammedans were victorious.

The above story cannot stand any historical test. The Kamadhaja Rāi mentioned in it is a fictitious name, inasmuch as we know of no individual of that name in history. Similarly, the name of Jayachchandra's father was not Vijayapāla, but Vijayachandra, who lived not in the beginning of the twelfth century of the Vikrama era, but in the first half of the thirteenth

1 According to the 'Rāsō' Pṛithvīrāja had died at an age of 43; so the date of this event comes to V.S. 1158.

century, as is evident from his copper plate grants[1] and inscriptions of V.S. 1224 and 1225. Again, although the period of Anangapāla has not yet been precisely ascertained, yet this much is certain that Somēshvara's third ancestor Vigraharāja (or Vīsaladēva IV) had acquired possession of Delhi, which is borne out by the inscription[2] of V. S. 1220 (A.D. 1163) on the pillar of Firōz Shah at Delhi. Under these circumstances, we do not understand how Sōmēshvara could have gone to Delhi to help Anangapāla. Moreover, in the "Pṛithvīrājavijaya Mahākāvya," which was written in Pṛithvīrāja's time, the name of Pṛithvīrāja's mother is mentioned not as Kamalāvatī, but as Karpūradēvī,[3] who is stated to be the daughter not of Tuṇvara Anangapāla, but of a king of the Haihaya dynasty (of Tripuri). In the "Hammīra Mahākāvya" also the name of Prithvīrāja's mother is mentioned as Karpūradēvī. The author of the "Rāsō" has mentioned the date of the birth of his hero Pṛithvīrāja[4] as V. S. 1115, but in fact Pṛithvīrāja should have been born in V.S. 1217 (A. D. 1160) or somewhat later, as at the death of his father in about V.S. 1236 (A.D. 1179) he was a minor and his mother took charge of the administration.

Let us now consider the tale of Pṛithvīrāja having married a daughter of Nāhaḍa Rāo, king of Maṇḍōr. This, too, is an absurdity, because from an incription of V. S. 894 of king Bāuka, who was tenth in descent from this Nāhaḍa Rāo, we conclude that the latter must have lived about V. S. 714, *i.e.*, nearly 500 years before Pṛithvīrāja. Sometime between V. S. 1189 and V. S. 1200 the Pratihāra

1 Kielhorn's Supplement to Northern List (Epigraphia Indica, Vol. VIII, Appendix I), page 18.

2 Epigraphia Indica, Vol. XIX, page 218.

3 Journal Royal Asiatic Society, (1913) page 275 f.

4 The names of Pṛithvīrāja's ancestors mentioned in the 'Rāsō' appear also to a large extent incorrect.

dynasty of Maṇḍōr had ceased to exist, having been overthrown by Chauhāna Rāyapāla, whose son Sahajapāla ruled at Maṇḍōr about V.S. 1200, as appears from his inscription found at Maṇḍōr.[1] Besides this, the name of the prime ancestor of the Paḍihāra dynasty of Kanauj was also Nāgabhaṭa (or Nāhaḍa). From the copper grant[2] dated V.S. 813 of the Chauhāna king Bhartṛivaḍḍha II, found at Hānsot, it appears that this Nāhaḍa lived in the beginning of the ninth century of the Vikram era. Further, the first Paḍihāra conqueror of Kanauj, too, was Nāgabhaṭa (Nāhaḍa II), who was fifth in descent from the aforesaid Nāhaḍa. He had died in V.S. 890, as appears from the "Prabhāvakacharitra." No fourth Nāhaḍa besides these has been heard of in the history of India.

We have already mentioned above V.S. 1217 as the approximate birth year of Pṛithvīrāja. In such a case, it would certainly be impossible to assume that Anangapāla made over the kingdom of Delhi to Pṛithvīrāja in V.S. 1138.

Further, the story of Pṛithvīrāja having abducted the daughter of the Yādava king Bhāṇa of Dēōgiri and of the consequent battle between Pṛithvīrāja and Jayachchandra, also seems to be spurious. The founder of the city of Dēōgiri, was not Bhāṇa, but Bhillama, who had founded the city about V.S. 1244 (A.D. 1187). Neither does this event find place in the history of Bhillama nor does the name Bhāṇa occur in the pedigree of the dynasty. Similarly, Vīrachandra, the name of a nephew of king Jayachchandra, occurs only in the 'Rāsō' and nowhere else.

We have mentioned above that an ancestor, third from Pṛithvīrāja's father, had acquired possession of Delhi. Thus, the talk of Tunvara Anangapāla's effort to regain his kingdom from Pṛithvīrāja on complaint from his subjects about the latter's high-handedness is an untenable proposition.

1 Archæol. Surv. Ind., An. Rep., 1909-10, pages 102-103.
2 Epigraphia Indica, Vol. XII, page 197.

There now remains the affairs of the 'Rājasūya' and 'Svayaṁvara' ceremonies performed by king Jayachchandra. Had Jayachchandra performed such a grand ceremony as the 'Rājasūya,' some mention of it would have been found in the inscriptions of that monarch, or in the 'Rambhāmaṇjarī Nāṭikā' by Nayachandra Sūri, of which Jāyachchandra himsēlf is the hero. Fourteen copper plates and two stone inscriptions[1] of Jayachchandra have been found, the last of which is dated V. S. 1245[2] (A. D. 1189). Although there are, thus, as many as sixteen epigraphic records belonging to him, not one of them contains any reference to his having celebrated a 'Rājasūya'

The story of Prithvīrāja's elopement with Saṁyōgitā seems to be a creation of the fertile brain of the author of the 'Rāso'. Neither the "Prithvīrājavijaya Mahākāvya" written in Prithvīrāja's time, nor the "Hammīra Mahākāvya" complied in the last half of the fourteenth century of the Vikrama era,[3] makes any mention of any such event. To rely on the story under these circumstances, is to tread on uncertain ground. The dates[4] of the events given in the "Rāsō" are alike incorrect.

The story of Mahārāvala Samarasingh of Mēwār being a brother-in-law of Prithvīrāja, and being killed

1 'Bhārata ke-Prāchīna Rājavaṁsha', part III, pp. 108-110.

2 Annual report of the Arch. Survey of India (1921-22). Pages 120-121.

3 Further there is no trace of Somavamshī Mukundadēva of Kaṭaka in the history of that period, whose daughter is mentioned as the mother of Saṁyōgitā in the 'Rāsō.'

4 Mr. Mōhan Lāl Vishṇu Lāl Pāṇḍyā had, however, assumed the dates of the 'Rāsō' to be based on the 'Ananda Vikrama Samvat,' which he takes for granted on the basis of the words 'विक्रमसाक अनंद' According to this the Vikrama Samvat is arrived by adding 91 to the Samvat stated in the 'Rāsō'. Thus, by adding 91 to the Samvat 1158, the date of Prithvīrāja's death arrived at according to the 'Rāsō,' we come to 1249. This date alone can be proved to be correct by this method. But the other dates and the periods assigned to Nāhaḍa Rāo, etc., still remain quite unreliable.

in the battle with Shahābuddīn, while helping his brother-in-law Pṛithvīrāja, is also an idle tale. This battle had, in fact, been fought in V. S. 1249, whereas Mahārāvala Samarasingh died in V. S. 1359. Under these circumstances, the above statement of the 'Rāsō' cannot be admitted as either true or possible.

After this, there is the mention of Pṛithvīrājā's son Raiṇasī, but in fact the name of Pṛithvīrāja's son was Gōvindarāja.[1] He being a child, his uncle Harirāja had usurped his dominion of Ajmer, whereupon Qutbuddīn, having defeated Harirāja, had protected Gōvindarāja.

In the end, there is the mention of an invasion by Qutbuddīn against Jayachchandra, but, according to the Persian histories of India, this invasion is said to have been made not after Shahābuddīn's death, but in his lifetime, and that he himself had taken part in it. He was killed at the hands of the Gakkhars in V. S. 1262 (A.D. 1206). Besides, in the Persian chronicles there is no mention of Jayachchandra's collusion with Shahābuddīn.

When all these circumstances are taken into consideration, the historical value of the "Pṛithvīrāja Rāsō" becomes vitiated. Besides, even if we accept for a moment the whole story of the 'Rāso' as correct, yet nowhere in that work is there any mention either of Jayachchandra having invited Shahābuddin to attack Pṛithvīrāja or of his having any other sort of connection whatsoever, with the Muhammedan ruler. On the other hand, at various places in the 'Rāsō' we read of Pṛithvīrāja's aggressive attacks, his elopement with the princess, his neglect of state affairs through his devotion to Samyōgitā, his proud and overbearing behaviour towards his brave and wise general Chāmuṇḍa Rāi, whom he had sent to prison without any fault on his part, and his high-handedness which gave rise to the complaints of the subjects of a state left as a legacy to him by his maternal grandfather. Along with this, we also learn from the 'Rāsō' that his unwise steps obliged his own generals to conspire with his enemy Sultan Shahābuddīn. In the light of these circumstances, readers will be able to judge for themselves how far it is just to dub king Jayachchandra with the title of Vibhīshaṇa and thus malign him as a traitor.

Let us now examine the attack made on Rāo Sīhā, grandson of Mahārāja Jayachchandra. Colonel James Tod[1] writes:—

"Here in the land of Kher amidst the sandhills of Luni (the salt-river of the desert) from which the Gohils were expelled, Sihaji planted the standard of the Rathors.

"At this period a community of Brahmans held the city and extensive land about Pali, from which they were termed Pallivals, and being greatly harassed by the incursions of the mountaineers, the Mers and Minas, they called in the aid of Sihaji's band, which readily undertook and executed the task of rescuing the Brahmans from their depredations. Aware that they would be renewed, they offered Sihaji lands to settle amongst them, which he readily accepted."

"Afterwards he found an opportunity to obtain land by putting to death the heads of this community and adding the districts to his conquests."

From the above history it is evident that before rendering aid to these Pallīvāla Brāhmaṇas, Rāo Sīhā had acquired possession of Mēhvā and Khēḍa. It does not seem reasonable that an adventurer, hankering after land, should have renounced possession of

1 Annals and Antiquities of Rajasthana, Vol. I. p p. 942-943.

these two large districts, merely to content himself with a few acres of land granted to him by his proteges, the Pallīvālas. Further, he had not at that time enough men with him to look after his posessions of Khēḍa and Mēhvā as well as for keeping under subjection the Mēras and Mīṇās of the hilly tracts, who often overran Pālī. Besides, from the narratives of the old chronicles of Mārwār we learn that the Pallīvālas of Pālī were a class of rich traders. It is nowhere recorded that they were masters of the town of Pālī; nor do we find any mention that Rāo Sīhā had murdered them. In the temple of Sōmanātha at Pālī, there is a stone inscription[1] of V.S. 1209 of Sōlankī Kumārapāla, which shows that at that time the latter held sway over Pālī. It also appears from this inscription that one Bāhaḍadēva, probably, a Chauhāna feudatory of Kumārapāla ruled over Pālī at this time on behalf of Kumārapāla. There had also been one Ālhaṇadēva, a Chauhāna feudatory and favourite of king Kumārapāla. An inscription[2], dated V.S. 1209, of Kirāḍu shows that this Ālhaṇadēva had acquired possession of the districts of Kirāḍu, Rāḍadhaḍā and Shiva by the favour of king Kumārapāla.[3]

On the death of Kumārapāla, about V.S. 1230, his nephew Ajayapāla succeeded to the throne. From this time the power of the Sōlankīs began to decline. Presumably, the Mīṇās and Mēras might have taken advantage of this weakness and plundered Pālī, which was then one of the richest cities in the vicinity. In the inscription dated V. S. 1319 at Sūndhā of Chauhāna Chāchigadēva it is stated that Udayasimha, father of Chāchigadēva, and great grandson of the aforesaid Ālhaṇadēva, was master of the districts of Nāḍol,

1 Annual report of the Archaeological Deptt., Jodhpur State, Vol. VI, (1931-32)p. 7.
2 „ „ „ „ „ „ „ Vol. IV, (1929-30)p. 7.
3 *Ep. Ind.*, Vol. XI, p. 70.

Jālōr, Maṇḍōr, Bāhaḍmer, Ratanapur, Sānchōr, Sūrāchand, Rāḍadhaḍā, Khēḍa Rāmsīn, and Bhīnmāl. Udayasiṁha is also described in this inscription as invincible to the kings of Gujrāt.[1] We have found four inscriptions of this king ranging from V. S. 1262 to V.S. 1306 at Bhīnmāl. We conclude, therefore, that at some time in this period, this Chauhān feudatory might have thrown off the yoke of the Sōlankī kings of Gujrāt. At the same time, when we consider the geographical position of the above-mentioned districts, we are led to believe that the city of Pālī, too, must have passed into the possession of the Chauhānas from the Sōlankīs. So that at the time of Rāo Sīhā's arrival in Mārwāṛ, such an important city as Pālī must have either been in possession of the Sōlankīs or the Chauhānas. What circumstances, then, could have obliged Rāo Sīhā to butcher his helpless and trading supplicants of the Brāhmaṇas, a caste so sacred to a Rājpūt for the possession of Pālī ?

Besides this, when finding themselves too weak to ward off the marauding incursions of the hill tribes, these Brāhmaṇas had themselves applied to Rāo Sīhā for help, and having gained experience of his prowess, and having appointed him to be their protector, how could they have ever dared to incur his wrath by an act of effrontery ?

Thus automatically Sīhā became master of the city, and so his interest lay in fostering its trade by conferring favours upon its merchants, the Pallīvāla Brāhmaṇas, and not in laying waste the country by killing these traders, as is supposed by the learned scholar, Colonel Tod.

---

1 *Ep. Ind.*, Vol. IX, p. 78, v. 46.

INDEX.

H

I

J

K

ERRATA.

PAGE.	LINE.	INCORRECT.	CORRECT.
3	30	Vishṇu vardhna	Vishṇuvardhana
8	22	Samvta	Samvat
8	28	Mohmedan	Mohammedan
10	33	Kakkala	Raṭṭarāja
10	35	300	298
11	27	वरग	वर्ग
15	28	Badāūn	Chandrāvatī
16	7	son	grandson
20	4	Rāyapāla	Rājypāla
21	12	Budhist	Buddhist
23	7 & 16	Budhist	Buddhist
29	36	x40	940
30	10	Vigyānēshvara	Vijnānēshvara
30	37	Saundarān *d* Mahā-kāvya, Sar *a*	Saundarānanda Mahākāvya, Sarga I
36	2	सदलङ्कृति	सदलङ्कृतिः
36	27	Budhist	Buddhist
40	14	kukam	Kukam
40	27	Dhruvarāja I	Dhruvarāja
44	6	Tivali	Ṭivili
44	18	Madnapāla	Madanapāla
44	22	Madnavarmadēva	Madanavarmadēva
45	9	Rāashṭrakūṭas	Rāshṭrakūṭas
53	6	Pulakēshīn II	Pulakēshin II
57	33	Bhavna	Bhavana
59	5	acended	ascended
59	10	Krisṇarāja	Krishṇarāja
61	32	Chakrāyudh	Chakrāyudha
65	33	Epigraphii	Epigraphia
67	20	Raṇṇādēv,ī	Raṇṇadēvī,
68	13	Trivali	Ṭivili
69	6	The Pulla Shakti	Pulla Shakti
75	2	Kapḍavanja	Kapaḍavanjā
75	3	geneological	genealogical
75	14	Krishṇa=	Krishṇa—
75	35-36	Vijayāditya III who killed king Mangi (son of Vishṇuvar-dhana V, of the Ganga dynasty)	Vijayāditya III (son of Vishṇuvardhana V), who killed king Mangi,

PAGE.	LINE.	INCORRECT.	CORRECT.
82	31	the Satyavākya *o*	Satyavākya
86	25	th	This
87	18	०कन्दुक०	०कुन्दक०
87	21	Kan—	Kun—
92	28	Pēremānaḍi *o*	Pēramānaḍio
95	19	rebellous	rebellious
96	13	weilded	wielded
98	1	Dhruvarāja, II	Dhruvarāja II,
98	3	Dantivarman I,	Dantivarman,
116	9	from.	From
127	34, 36 & 43	Qutubuddīn	Qutbuddīn
128	20	(Panjab)	(Punjab)
128	27	desparate	desperate
129	22 & 24	Qutubuddīn	Qutbuddīn
134	21	Vijaypāla	Vijayapāla
134	21	Rāhṭhōḍa	Rāṭhōḍa
136	13	disorgani—	the disorgani—

ERRATA (II)

Page	Line	Incorrect	Correct
Preface	22	Gōvindachandra	Madanapāla
2	26	4	44.
12	5	872	782.
16	7	son	grand-son.
19	31-32	coppergrant	inscription.
29	36	940	894.
54	6	of the Sōlankīs found at Miraj.	found at Miraj of the Sōlankīs
66	6	(V. S. 870 = A. D. 813)	(V. S. 8[illegible] = A. D. 812).
66	19	Kadamba	Kadaba.
68	15	Gōvinda II	Dhruvarāja.
74	35	22	220.
84	11	845	945.
85	29	No. 89	No. 99.
89	35	प्रजापार्जित	प्रतापजित
92	23	Do. No. 12	Grand son of No. 12.
92	23	858	838.
95	33	156	158.
96	1	870	869.
96	2	813	812.
109	6	Arjunavarman	Ajavarman.
118	6	Naynpāla	Nayanapāla.
120	33	वसन्तदेवी	वसन्तदेव्या:
131	22	Bījāpur	Bijaipur
131	25	प्रतापगढ़नामा	फतैहगढ़नामा
131	37	Ganges	Kālī.
145	32	Bhāṭī 13	Bhāṭī 31.
148	24	Gold	Silver

ERRATA (III).

Page.	Line.	Incorrect.	Correct.
7	24		*Foot Note:*—But some people are of opinion that Laṭalūrpur may be Lāṭūr of Deccan.
31	6	देवराजोऽयं	देवराजं यो
36	25	All	Most of
36	28	only	×
36	30	for the first time	×
45	27		*Foot Note:*—The migration of Sihaji might be due to the pressure of Shamsuddin, the Governor of Badaun. (Chronology of India, p. 176)
45	32	there	there. (Vol. II, p. 507).
46	25	8th	9th
46	26	9th	10th
61	17-18	Vatsarāja of 'Avanti' in the east; and Varāha in the west.	Avanti-King in the east; Vatsarāja in the west; and Varāha (Jaya-varāha in 'Sōramandal' (Gujrat).
62	9	North.	West.
63	19-20	the ruler.....(Cambay).	Yuvarāja.
65	3-4	(Coimbatur)	×
65	35	Unpublished grant.	Epigraphia Indica, Vol. XVIII, p. 243-251
66	6	(V. S. 870=A. D. 813)	(V. S. 869=A. D. 812)
69	37-38	unpublished	×
70	15-16	unpublished	×
71	18	Western.	Eastern
77	8	Vāsudēva,	Vasudēva,
86	4	drama	book
95	1	Two	Four
			Third of S. 743 (V. S. 878=A. D. 821). (Ep. Indica, Vol. XXI, p. 140-146). Fourth of S. 746 (V. S. 881=A.D. 824). (found at Brāhmaṇapalli)
99	13	734 & 738	734, 738, 743, & 746.
111	10	Pratihāra	Paramāra
111	33	Pratihāra	Paramāra
118	12	Mumdaliya	Mamdaliya
131	6		*Foot Note:*—The migration of Sihaji might be due to the pressure of Shamsuddin Altamash, the Governor of Badaun. (Chronology of India, p. 176)
145	38	13	31.
147	11	92	92, 52.
149	25	63	53, 63,